T0355411

Recasting Public Administration in India

Recasting Public Administration in India

Reform, Rhetoric, and Neoliberalism

Kuldeep Mathur

OXFORD
UNIVERSITY PRESS

OXFORD
UNIVERSITY PRESS

Oxford University Press is a department of the University of Oxford.
It furthers the University's objective of excellence in research, scholarship,
and education by publishing worldwide. Oxford is a registered trademark of
Oxford University Press in the UK and in certain other countries.

Published in India by
Oxford University Press
2/11 Ground Floor, Ansari Road, Daryaganj, New Delhi 110 002, India

© Oxford University Press 2019

The moral rights of the author have been asserted.

First Edition published in 2019

ISBN-13 (print edition): 978-0-19-949035-6
ISBN-10 (print edition): 0-19-949035-X

ISBN-13 (eBook): 978-0-19-909702-9
ISBN-10 (eBook): 0-19-909702-X

Typeset in Bembo Std 10.5/13
by The Graphics Solution, New Delhi 110 092
Printed in India by Rakmo Press, New Delhi 110 020

Contents

Introduction

Ever since a democratic system of government was adopted and a strategy of planned economic development launched in India, there have been doubts about the capacity of the government system to respond to the demands of the new environment. As democracy was taking shape, people's aspirations were rising after a long struggle for freedom that gave them an opportunity to break away from the shackles of poverty and deprivation. But this task was not easy. British colonial rule had left behind many legacies that militated against the pursuit of a new social and economic order. Among them was the system of colonial administration and a civil service that exuded arrogance and self-confidence for its ability to carry out any task that was demanded of it. However, many were sceptical of its abilities, and Nehru himself had famously declared that 'no new order could be built in India so long as the spirit of Indian Civil Service [British civil service that had come to be identified with imperialist rule] pervades our administration and our public services' (quoted in Potter 1986: 2).

The planners themselves were quite conscious of the need for a different administrative system to implement the planned objective of development and wrote so in several chapters of plan documents. The government responded to this concern by appointing a number of committees to suggest changes in the system. Even before the beginning of the planning era, N. Gopalaswami Ayyangar had prepared a report on the central government as early as 1949 and this was soon followed by a report for the Planning Commission by A.D. Gorwala in 1951.Very early in the journey of democracy and development, international experts were invited to join in this endeavour of changing the administrative system. In 1953, Paul Appleby, a professor at Syracuse University in the United States, was brought in as a consultant and his report 'Public Administration in India' did much to raise hope about administrative reform. More reports and committees followed and national concerns culminated in the appointment of the high-level Administrative Reforms Commission in 1966. Scores of recommendations spread in innumerable reports were presented. It is a matter of debate whether these efforts at reform over the first two decades of India's independence made any substantive impact on the practice of public administration in India. Reports on improving the implementation of poverty alleviation programmes during the 1970s and 1980s continued to chant the same litany of complaints of an ineffective administration and offer as many suggestions to reform it. Paradoxically, as these criticisms grew, strength in the resilience of the colonial administrative system and its legacy of civil service also rose and survived to perpetuate itself.

It does appear that after this effort, the government, more or less, gave up on reform. The period from 1980s onwards did not even have symbolic committees to look into issues of reform. This also marked the beginning of the period when policies to liberalize the economy were initiated. With liberalization, demands on administration assumed different contours. The concern about reform and change was revived in the context of liberalization when the Second Administrative Reforms Commission was established around 40 years after the first one in 1966. The years of neglect allowed the administrative system to further entrench itself in its old traditional ways and to develop strength to withstand any challenges from outside. The theory and practice of administration had also changed in response to the new policy thrusts of liberalization and globalization. International consultants who as reform had proposed development administration as the panacea for the traditional one now came calling with governance reform proposing the adoption of private managerial practices in public administration and reaching out to the private sector for implementing public policy goals became the new mantra.

If the plan period lasting for around 30 years saw an effort to strengthen state intervention as a recipe for triggering development, the 1980s ended with disastrous accounts of the failures of interventionist and regulatory actions. Efforts to dismantle state machinery and to transform its role now began. The state acknowledged its failure to provide for improved delivery of public goods and services, and began to look to the private sector and other non-government actors for support in framing state policies and implementing them. The story of administration as an impediment to development took a drastic turn with the introduction of neoliberal economic reforms and the acceptance of the concept of governance to transform government.

The conventional world of public administration was shaken with calls for adopting management practices of the private sector and to interact with it to achieve goals that were seen as its sole responsibility. Ideas from Western practices and mechanisms to improve the performance of public administration began to attract Indian reformers once again. The fundamental basis of these ideas, subsumed under the broad umbrella of governance reform, were based on the premise that public and private administration are basically the same—the notion of generic management (Peters 2003: 7). It was thus possible to adopt private management practices in public administration. In addition, it was also accepted within this framework that the role of the state was to enable the market to take over as many functions as needed to dismantle the government itself.

Neoliberalism began to give rise to a new vocabulary in the discourse of public administration through its advocacy of governance reforms. This vocabulary has little to do with hierarchy, bureaucracy, neutrality, or demarcating institutional boundaries. What is emerging are notions such as policy communities, network relationships, regulating agencies, semi-autonomous government agencies, and so on. As Miller and Fox (2007: 134) point out, the foundations that grounded public administration have now become diffused.

This book proposes to provide a window to the efforts at government reform and the challenges that the Indian public administration faces as ideas from Western theory and practices get imbibed by policy planners in India. Eager to receive international financial investment and technology, India is also becoming a recipient of managerial ideas whose efficacy is yet to be tested on Indian soil. New institutions are being layered on traditional ones, and a fresh Leviathan, at best, an incoherent one, appears to be emerging.

In making public administration more effective in delivering public services, governance reform has meant accepting the idea that private sector is a partner in the process and not a separate entity. Privatizing the mode of delivery is an alternative way to make the goals of public administration more achievable. In this framework, the concept of public–private partnership (PPP) has emerged as an institution that will combine public interest with private sector efficiency and management skills.

We propose to elucidate the emergence of such PPPs as institutional innovations with special reference to the social sector and the changes that they demand in the larger context of the prevailing system of public administration. The following chapters will examine the reform effort and the reasons for which it did not bear much fruit. However, policymakers seem to be more receptive to institutional ideas recommended within the neoliberal perspective. As development policy becomes more complex, it may not be easy to continue with conventional public administration, on the one hand, and a new architecture of administration inspired by neoliberalism and new public management, on the other. Governments all over the world have the responsibility to provide some basic goods and services. These include security, law and order, land administration, public finance management, and so on. To expect that unreformed public administration can carry out these tasks effectively and efficiently while new governance institutions can carry on with the business of pursuing development is most probably an unsustainable proposition (Pritchette et al. 2010).

In addition, the new neoliberal world needs the state, and an effective one at that. Contrary to popular belief and perceptions, state assumes a critical role. It is needed to help sustain its key institution of markets. Markets are spaces in which competition takes place between suppliers and customers such that there is choice regarding opportunities for exchange. At the core is the promotion of markets and competition for bringing about greater efficiency and economy in the delivery of public services. As long as two parties act in their own self-interest and have multiple parties to carry out exchanges with, the outcome will be increase in welfare. If any party of either suppliers or consumers is able to set the resulting price through free exchange arbitrarily, it will be a case of market failure (Davies 2014: 39). Rise of neoliberalism was precisely a response to state intervention through economic planning of these competitive processes that lead to price fixation and market failure. The movement against the state had developed on this basis and the assumption was that lessening or doing away with the planning process will lead to greater public welfare. But the state was still needed to see that competition was free and fair; therefore, the movement did not seek to shrink the state but to transform it.

As this ideology began to pan out, rules of free competition and free market began to be formulated. For it was found that there were ways in which suppliers and consumers could develop competitive strategies that could lead to unfair practices. If liberal thought was based on free competition and laws of supply and demand, it began to be realized that it was possible to understand and influence the environment in which business functioned. This understanding considerably moulded the relationship between business and government. As Davies (2014) points out, on the one hand, it led to the rise of professionals, managers, consultants, and academics to aid business, and on the other, it made the governments realize that they needed effective public institutions that could respond to such influence of business. The central question then became how public policy and public institutions could be oriented and strengthened to ensure this. Strengthening public institutions was now of interest to both the state as well as business.[1]

But reforming public administration is not limited to introducing new public–private institutions alone. Administrative reform is still needed to provide a unity of purpose for both to work together. We contend that it is unrealistic to expect that new governance institutions and conventional administration that is widely accepted to have failed in its routine responsibility can function effectively side by side. But this is the experiment that is being tried in India and presents a challenge that we need to explore further.

---

[1] Voices are being raised about how administrative reforms are needed in the conventional public administration in India. The governor of Reserve Bank of India stated publicly in 2015: 'It has often been said that India is a weak state. Not only are we accused of not having the administrative capacity of ferreting out wrong doing, we do not punish the wrong doer—unless he is small and weak…. . If we are to have strong sustainable growth, the culture of impunity has to stop' (quoted in *Hindustan Times* 19 January 2015).

1 Administrative System

Early Assessment

Concern about reforming public administration in India is not something new. Efforts began with the initiation of a development strategy in the early 1950s whose main goal was to alleviate poverty. The colonial administration that existed at the time of Independence was not seen as conducive to the implementation of this strategy. India began to search for ideas for reform and opened up to international academics and consultants for fresh thinking. The entry of American experts and technocrats into the Planning Commission in the early 1950s had signalled India's openness to foreign expertise in the field of development policy. India also turned to such experts for advice on how to improve or transform its administrative system. Rosen (1985) has documented the close relationship that existed between Western policymakers and economists in the newly created Planning Commission. He has also shown how programmes of collaboration intended to affect policy and create new institutions or strengthen existing ones. Such openness also paved the way for the introduction of American ideas of public administration reform to Indian policymakers.

Thus, the planning strategy gained lot of prestige as the views of Indian and Western experts merged to celebrate India's bold attempt at alleviating poverty. Consequently, when plan goals were not achieved, the focus turned to the impediments created by an inherited bureaucratic and administrative system of the British colonial days and not towards any investigation in the weakness in the planning process itself. This focus found expression in demands for the need of a different system to implement the planned objectives of development, and planners themselves wrote so in chapters of several plan documents. The government responded to this concern by appointing many committees to suggest changes in the system. During the 1950s these efforts bore the imprint of analysis of administrative problems by American experts whom the academic fraternity and policy planners in India welcomed with open arms. In this expression of concern for administrative reform, public administration emerged as an academic discipline in India and provided the intellectual background for suggestions to improve public administration in practice. Intellectual analysis of the problems of public administration and the nature of efforts at administrative reform are closely linked.

THE COLONIAL LEGACY

The design of public administration in India with its attendant feature of a civil service that dominated all its operations has been the lasting legacy of the British colonial rule. The critical institution that dispensed law and order and justice was the district administration headed by a district collector, also known as district magistrate. He was responsible for revenue collection, maintaining land records, and resolving disputes among local population. The size of a district was usually very large and the district manager had to travel a lot in his domain to discharge his functions. This enabled him to impart instant justice and resolve disputes. The district was part of a province headed by a governor, who, in turn, reported to the governor general at the Centre. The distances between the Centre and the periphery were great and communication lines were time consuming, allowing field officers—district collectors—to be masters of their domain. They represented the Crown and were seen as such. In this structural set-up, district administration was the critical unit where all the ramifications of colonial rule were seen and felt.

This administrative structure was held together by the Indian Civil Service (ICS). From 1862, when it was formed, it was staffed by the British, and Indians were precluded from joining it by the rules framed for its recruitment and training. The ICS was recruited and trained in London, and its members, for the most part, had studied at the universities of Oxford and Cambridge. Their service conditions and rules of appointment were determined by the secretary of state in London and they owed allegiance to the imperial government and not to the colonial government under whom they served in India. This was a crucial factor that gave them the opportunity of rising above local political and social pressures and the veneer of impartiality and neutrality. Thus, it was possible for the ICS to see themselves above civil society, above the conflicts of caste and communities, and acquire an image of what later came to be known as that of 'guardians'.

For the British rulers, the ICS was the 'steel frame' that held the colonial rule together. Speaking in the British Parliament in 1922, then Prime Minister Lloyd George, referring to the ICS as steel frame, said: 'If you take the steel frame out of the fabric, it would collapse. There is one institution that we will not cripple, there is one institution we will not deprive of its functions and privileges, and that is the institution which built up the British Raj—the British Indian Civil Service of India' (quoted in Maheshwari 1992: 26). London lauded its imperial role and Indians held the service in awe.

It was this design that came to be known as the legacy of colonial rule and was celebrated through what came to be known ICS mythology. The building blocks for the creation of this mythology were provided by the contribution of many British administrators themselves, mainly belonging to the ICS. Many of these contributions were in the nature of memoirs, and apart from being descriptive of the customs and manners of Indian society, they were also rich in detail about the workings of the British Indian administration, creating a romantic view of field administration. One of the premier representatives of the most romanticized version of the role of the ICS is *The Guardians*, the second volume of Philip Woodruff's well-known study *The Men Who Ruled India* (1954). Even though Woodruff asserted that the term 'guardians' was his own, several writers (ex-civil servants) joined him in perpetuating the myth of the altruistic characteristics of the ICS, in which platonic guardianship and men of superior virtue dominated. The love of outdoor life, commitment to the district and the welfare of its population, courage and daring in decision-making, independence, and integrity were among the many other virtues that the ICS seemed to possess. The Indian members of the ICS helped in perpetuating these myths through their own writings in the post-Independence era (Chettur 1964; Punjabi 1965).[1]

A number of scholars, particularly British, also joined in this chorus. A rhetorical question like the following was asked: 'How is it, that 760 British members of the ruling Indian Civil Service could as late as 1939, in the face of the massive force of India's national movement led by Gandhi, held down 378 million Indians?' (Spangenburg 1976: 4). Such a question implied that the British had the skills to govern India. This assertion was based on three essential myths: (*i*) the myth of the popularity of the civil service as a profession that attracted the best minds, (*ii*) the myth of efficiency in administering India, and (*iii*) the myth of sacrificial esprit de

---

[1] Some members of the IAS, the service that followed the ICS, helped in perpetuating these myths through their own writings in the post-Independence era. See their reminiscences of IAS in Dar (1998) and Arora (2015).

corps of the ICS, which ostensibly infused the government with the primary concern of working for the welfare of the people.

For the British, the perpetuation of this myth served many functions. It came as a defence of British imperialism in the court of world public opinion. Teddy Roosevelt, at the end of his second term as president in 1909, cited British administration in India as a prime example of overwhelming advancement achieved as a result of white or European rule among the 'peoples who dwell in the darker corners of the earth' (Spangenberg 1976: 7). It also helped assuage internal opinion in England, reassuring the British ruling classes that the British rule was beneficial to India.

This assurance to the British ruling classes as well as world public opinion was important for the moral justification of British colonial rule. Drawing a distinction between local colonial administration and an imperial government in London, Mukherjee (2010) has argued that the British Empire, over the two centuries, was not a simple and homogenous phenomenon but rather a complex one. There were two competing but collaborating discourses: the discourse of the colonial and the discourse of the imperial. The discourse of colonial governance was driven by ideas of territorial conquest, power, violence, domination, and subjugation of the colonized. The imperial, on the other hand, was based on supranational de-territorialized discourse of justice under natural law and was critical and censorial towards the arbitrary exercise of power by the colonial government. Colonial interests often came into conflict with the imperial ones. From this argument, it is possible to surmise that the ICS, which came after the British government took over to rule India directly after 1857, derived its role not from that of the colonial administration but from the concerns of the imperial government. It was a 'covenanted' civil service whose recruitment and service conditions were determined by the secretary of state in London. The ICS were more often than not seen as serving imperial interests of justice. Its members saw themselves as separate from civil society, above conflicts of local castes and communities, and thus cultivated an attitude of neutrality and being above society. This is what led others to label them as 'heaven born' and the appellate 'guardians' began to be attached to them. Because the imperial interests saw India as a political configuration of warring communities, it needed an outside civil service to rule over it and dispense law and order and justice. The ICS fulfilled the role. This was probably the cultural capital that helped the ICS build its image.

This myth not only survived but also prospered many years after Independence. The basic framework of administration continued way after Independence as if the colonial administrators had not departed at all. As an Indian journalist later remarked, 'This would be unbelievable were it not true' (Potter 1986: 2). Nehru and his colleagues sought to build 'a new India, a more egalitarian society ... through the agency of those who had been the trained servants of imperialism' (quoted in Potter 1986: 2). What is paradoxical is that this myth persisted well after Independence and even when it was seen to be an impediment in creating a new society.

The inability of national leadership to bring about change in the early 1950s set the old system of administration in firm saddle. Nehru writing much before Independence had said, 'I am quite sure that no new order can be built up in India so long as the spirit of the ICS pervades our administration and our public services. That spirit of authoritarianism ... cannot exist with freedom... . Therefore, it seems essential that the ICS and similar services must disappear completely as such before we can start real work on a new order' (Nehru 1953: 8). However, when the issue of protecting the independence of the inherited civil services and its successor was debated in the Constituent Assembly, the home minister, Sardar Patel, stood up to defend their role and lauded their contribution in holding the country together. He also insisted that professional values and neutral advice was at the core of their role, which could only be elicited if some degree of independence from everyday political pulls and pressures was guaranteed to them. Thus, the successor, Indian Administrative Service (IAS), was provided constitutional guarantees to act in an independent fashion free of day-to-day political wranglings. In the spring of 1964, Nehru was asked at a private meeting with some friends what he considered to be his greatest failure as India's first prime minister. He reportedly replied, 'I could not change the administration, it is still colonial administration' (quoted in Potter 1986: 2). He went on to elaborate his belief that colonial administration was one of the main causes of India's inability to solve the problem of poverty.

The irony of Nehru's critical evaluation of the civil service of colonial days was that little attempt was made to change the character of the civil service that inherited its mantle from the colonial ICS. On the other hand, deliberate constitutional guarantees were given to sustain its role as a professional, neutral civil service mandated to carry out the policies set out by the political leadership in the image of the ICS. Chhotray (2012: 301) has suggested that political arrangements were such that Nehru was isolated in his own party and received little support for his views. Finding that his support was thinly dispersed among the elite in government and modern sectors, he turned to bureaucracy to carry out his vision of social transformation. The result was that the civil service, without shedding its pre-eminent role during colonial rule, now acquired a new significance that further embellished its pre-eminence in independent India.

The essential point is that the British colonial administration, upheld by its many myths, survived and entrenched itself well into the postcolonial period. However, the introduction of Community Development Programme first raised the demand of a new type of administrator who would be unrelated to the colonial one. The administrators began to be told that a programme of social change like that of community development could not be implemented successfully through colonial administrative structures and procedures. The administrators were exhorted to identify with rural life.

What is significant is that the demand for a new type of administrator was raised without any effort to change the administrative system. Ironically, the Community Development Programme was organized and designed bureaucratically, extending its outreach through a hierarchical chain that connected the ministry of Community Development in Delhi to the village-level worker. The district collector/magistrate also assumed the new function of becoming a district development officer heading a development hierarchy parallel to that of revenue administration. The first opportunity at an innovative and reform-oriented administration was thus lost.

2 Nature of Indian Administration

The Indian administrative system is based on a federal system of government. The Constitution provides for division of powers between the Centre and the states. In many ways, the division of powers gives pre-eminence to the Centre, making the federation lean towards a unitary system. The exact nature of powers that are divided and the way they are played out in practice determines the extent of centralization within the federal system. Political parties play a major role in shaping the interactions between the Centre and the states. As different political parties form governments at the Centre and in the states, differences arise. Most of the differences arise from the way financial resources are shared between the Centre and the states and how the Centre encroaches on the latter's domain through centrally financed development schemes. With time, many of these differences are getting ironed out.

Within this federal framework and its attendant ways of working, public administration in India is marked by two major characteristics. One, as in all parliamentary systems, there is a secretariat where the ministers sit with their civil service advisors making policies and giving directions to field administration. The minister is accountable to Parliament for all actions of his ministry, which include functions performed at the secretariat as well as the field level.

Classical understanding of the parliamentary system is that the secretariat with each department head as secretary to the government provides support and advice to the concerned minister who formulates policy. The secretariat is the service agency providing support in policymaking. In organizational terms, it is a staff agency. To perform this function, a system of procedures has been developed to support the secretary in giving policy advice. During the British days, the secretariat was small for various reasons. This small staff has considerably expanded resulting in a tall hierarchy—leading from a dealing assistant to the secretary who heads the department. Various levels have been added to allow for many heads to contribute to the solution of a problem. The result is that a file is created, which keeps on burgeoning as it moves upwards.

In an interesting citation of colonial legacy, Bagchi (2007: 366) traces the shaping of the file system to Lord Curzon. He decreed the use of file boards on which sheets of paper should be unfolded and laid upon each other as they are received. He prescribed that the file boards should have straps of 'stout tapes that were not flimsy or breakable' (Bagchi 2007: 366) to hold the file and papers together when they attain size and weight—which they invariably did. This was the origin of 'red-tapism', which Bagchi attributes to Viceroy Lord Curzon. With expansion in work, this system acquired its own inefficiencies. While delays in reaching a decision are common, multiple levels also provide opportunities for additional comments. These comments could intentionally or otherwise modify the background information and influence the nature of the decision taken.

The secretary invariably belongs to the IAS and reaches this post only after spending around 30 years on average in government service, rotating among a mix of jobs at the state level and the Centre. The person is usually nearing his age of retirement when he assumes this top position. Being promoted to secretary to the Government of India is considered the crowning achievement of a civil servant's career. For those aspiring for this position, denial means considerable headache and allegations of favouritism fly easily. Extensive administrative experience is required to rise in the hierarchy and reach the top position. For many, the rise in hierarchy may not be only due to acceptable performance but also because of extraneous factors such as having taken 'politically correct' decisions or having 'played safe' in career.

Field administration is headed by district collector, who acts as a representative of the government and is held responsible for all the multifarious functions performed at the district level—from revenue collection, resolution of land disputes, to law and order or development. The position of the district collector is crucial to the legacy of colonial administration since it has been left untouched in the democratic era. It is also the position that has been romanticized by the British as well as Indian civil servants, and forms the basis on which the mythology of 'guardians' has been created. In the colonial days, the functions at the field level were primarily those of revenue collection and maintaining law and order. The district collector also imparted justice and resolved disputes and held court as district magistrate. The district collector continues to perform these functions to this day.

The change that has taken place is that of continuous addition of duties and responsibilities to these core functions. Some of these changes had started taking place when the colonial administration had begun to introduce reforms in the early twentieth century. These additions, however, gained momentum once the independent country embarked on its developmental agenda. In the primary role, the district collector headed an administrative hierarchy that extends to the village level. In the additional functions, he was most often given the responsibility of playing a coordinating role. But he continued to be the spokesman and representative of the government at the district level for all the multifarious functions that began to be allotted to him. As development became the focus of the government, a distinction began to be made between revenue administration and development administration. The implementation of development programmes was now integral to development administration. For this segment, the district collector was designated as district development officer. When the Panchayati Raj was introduced in 1959 and later when it was given a Constitutional mandate, the district collector was again made responsible for its implementation and supervision. What is significant is that he continues to be responsible for the district in all its dimensions and in all emergencies, whether drought, famine, or flood, and is seen as representing the government.

Paradoxically, schemes of decentralization introduced after Independence tended to strengthen rather than weaken the role of the collector. When the Community Development Programme was introduced, a parallel development hierarchy was created with the collector—who was also designated as district magistrate—heading it. The territorial divisions established for the purpose of collecting revenue were now supplemented by those established to implement development programmes. The hierarchy of the revenue division began from the offices of the *patwari* (a revenue official at village level), *tehsildar* (a collection of villages known as *tehsils*), and subdivisional officer, extending up to the office of the district collector. In parallel development hierarchy rose from the village extension worker and block development officer to the district development officer, who was the collector. Vesting so much power in an individual meant that both political leadership at various levels and the government came to depend on him for information and performance.

With the passage of time, more and more development departments began to be added to district administration, adding to its complexity. Each of these departments maintained their hierarchy at the district level, but the collector continued to be designated as the sole officer responsible for all that happened at the district level. He was also frequently sought by these departments to use his authority to get their targets achieved. He is now responsible for coordinating the activities of all district departments and chairing multifarious interdepartmental meetings for this purpose. Called as the 'pivot of governance', the collector is the one-point contact for the Government of India and acts as its eyes and ears (Bagchi 2007). The district collector invariably belonged to the civil service— the same body to which his compatriots sat advising in the secretariat. Thus, accountability flowed upwards to colleagues of the same civil service. For most new recruits to the civil service, a stint in the district was necessary to grow in their careers. It was enjoined in the rules that the new entrant would be sufficiently grounded in district administration before moving up in the hierarchy, which may lead him to the coveted secretariat or its equivalent position. New entrants were also motivated to move out of the district for another reason. With expansion in district functionaries, many of the district functional officers were too experienced and senior in their career to accept the leadership of the young collector without hesitation. The democratic institutions and logic of local politics also demanded of collectors experience and maturity. Young entrants hardly had the mettle to face the multifarious challenges of the job. The result, on account of these and many other factors, has been that the tenure of collectors has been going down over the years, mostly because of their own volition. Another issue that has surfaced is the resentment among the functional district administrators for being led by a comparatively inexperienced and young officer. The role of the collector in this sense has weakened when for the colonial administration it was of prime importance.

The second characteristic of the inherited administrative system, with its attendant attributes, was having an All India Civil Service (ICS). This service serves the administration at all levels of government, central and state. Heads of districts, known as district collectors/magistrates/deputy commissioners, have to be members of this service to be appointed to these positions. It has survived even when the Indian Constitution has provided for a federal system of government. The fact that this service provides a direct link from the Centre to the districts has stood in good stead whenever the Centre wants to enforce its diktats. Thus, during the breakdown of law and order at the time of the Partition of the country, during the declaration of Emergency in 1975, or during national calamities where direction from the Centre is of paramount importance, a unified service has proved to be of enormous significance whereby directions can be issued directly to field administrators in the hope that they will be adhered to.

It was probably for this reason that the government of an independent India readily accepted to provide continuity to the ICS through the successor IAS without changing its basic character. The first Administrative Reforms Commission (ARC) report on personnel administration mentions that 'the main considerations for the formation of the IAS were to provide top administrative personnel to the central and state governments; to bring uniformity in the standards of administration throughout the country; to facilitate constant liaison between the Centre and the States; to provide central administrative machinery intimate contacts with grass-roots level' (quoted in Bagchi 2007: 23). This provided a continuity to the colonial ICS and was the reason why the British image of 'guardians' lingered on in the civil service. This lineage provided a special sense of calling that fortified IAS officers against the populist onslaughts of democratic politicians and the elected representatives and ministers who were their new masters. It also lingered on in the mistaken belief that amateur generalists were equipped to perform the technical and expert tasks involved in managing a vast and complex industrial and financial sector and to initiate rural development (Rudolph and Rudolph 2003: 268).

The traditional system of administration as inherited from the British provided simple solutions to governing a vast diversified country. The Weberian/Wilsonian hierarchical system allowed control of administration by the British rulers at the top while the Indians were to work at lower levels. In a command-and-control system, this was in perfect harmony with British imperial interests and Indian aspirations. What tightly bound the hierarchy was the introduction of a civil service manned by the British who held all crucial positions that determined policy and administrative action.[1]

Over the years, this structure entrenched itself. The IAS expanded as the state embarked on development tasks and came to rely on more and more of its members to fulfill its development goals. Laws multiplied and so did rules that guided administrative action.[2] Colonial rules of procedure continue to survive. As we have pointed out earlier, the feeling that administration was an impediment to development and not its instrument became stronger. In the traditional administrative system, rules create rigid routines and bureaucratic behaviour is structured around them; these rules, in turn, 'were interpretations of the past rather than anticipations of the future' (Fukuyama 2004: 107). Upward accountability and standardized procedures militate against flexibility and continuous interaction with society.

The IAS was recruited on the same model as the British ICS and also worked under its long shadow. An image of elitism was deliberately built into it to provide it a sense of separation from the common society. This was supported by frequent movement of officials from one position to another, and a few people, whirled about by rapid transfers, were propelled by automatic promotions into higher positions exclusively reserved for them at all levels of government.

A system of state cadres was accepted whereby IAS officers were allotted to states as per the requirement of the state. The number

---

[1] It was very difficult for Indians to compete for entry into the higher civil services as recruitment processes were conducted in London.

[2] Paradoxically, earlier rules of procedures survive and are tweaked but not changed to serve a particular case.

of IAS officers thus varied across states. But this allotment did not mean that they were under the administrative control of state governments. An elaborate system of disciplining recalcitrant officers was created, dividing the powers between the central government and the Union Public Service Commission, which was the recruiting agency. This was again meant to keep them independent of local politics.

Whatever reforms had been introduced to make the service more representative did not affect the basic formula of recruiting young college graduates from any field. These graduates would gain experience as they moved from one job to another in service. In this way, it was assumed that the members of the IAS would develop broader horizons of governance and not have the blinkered vision of a specialist. A career was assured so that they rose to the highest positions that the service offered. Holding near monopoly of secretariat positions and as heads of field administration as district collectors, they were close to their political masters in framing policy. The IAS is the glue to the Indian administrative system, providing coherence and legitimacy to it. Other groups of administrators look at it with envy and aspire to step on the same career ladder that leads to such command and positions of control and authority.[3]

Indeed, the practice of Indian administration cannot be understood without recognizing the place of the IAS in it. It draws its legacy from a civil service that was described as a 'steel frame' and from the powerful image of officers as guardians (Woodruff 1954). In everyday life, it imparted a sense of superiority to the civil servants who believed in their 'heaven born' status to rule over the common man. Young men and women aspire to become members of this service, and those who ace the recruitment examinations get a top billing in the media. Educational institutions (and now

---

[3] For their distribution among states cadres and their numbers, see Annexure 2.

coaching schools) and states to which the candidates belong take pride over the success of their candidates.[4]

The early period of planning and development was also the period when the state was extending its role in social and economic activities. If anything was happening, it was the proliferation of administrative agencies as the role of the state expanded. The participation of large public enterprises in the industrial sector and the introduction of community development programmes in the rural sector resulted in a vast expansion of bureaucracy. This expansion in bureaucracy and installation of bureaucrats from the civil service in key positions took place with the active support of the very political leadership that had at one point pleaded for complete transformation of colonial administration in independent India. Nehru looked at the support of the civil servants for implementing his strategy of industrialization and social change. Rudolph and Rudolph (1987: 77) have argued that 'as Nehru's co-authors and implementers civil servants were the vanguard for the lobby of an industrial strategy of collaborating for creation of basic and heavy industry under the second and third five year plans.... They were also its principal beneficiaries.' During his tenure most large enterprises were manned by civil servants, who rose to command high-level managerial positions in them. Becoming captains of public industries gave these officers tremendous prestige and power not only in relation to the private sector, but within the government sector. The leading advisors of Nehru and Indira Gandhi were civil servants, mostly of the ICS variety—Boothlingam in finance and steel; C.D. Deshmukh, Vishnu Sahay, and Tarlok Singh in planning; and H.V.R. Iyengar in commerce, to name a few (Mathur 1991). Bureaucratic power now meant not only regulation and control, but also establishment of a new class that was strongly associated with the state

[4] This is reflected in the data provided by the Union Public Service Commission on the applicants for examinations. See Annexure 3.

sector and prospered because of it. Civil servants had a strong stake in state institutions and their expansion.

Similar steps were undertaken in the rural sector. To implement the schemes of community development, a large bureaucratic hierarchy was created. This was also in keeping with the advice from international experts who tended to differentiate between development and traditional bureaucracy. This bureaucratic system again brought the IAS to man the key positions, who were then exhorted to work for the rural poor.

Failure of this developmental administrative system to implement the goals of community development was recognized when panchayats were established in 1957 to mobilize people's participation in development. There is considerable literature of those days, including government reports, that highlight the continuous conflicts between the panchayat system and the local bureaucracy and political leadership (see Mathur 2012 for a review). In most cases, the bureaucracy saw panchayats as encumbrances that had to be tolerated in implementing nationally directed development programmes. What was happening was that programmes to involve the people in making collective efforts for development usually resulted in domination by the administrative system, which suffocated people's participation (Government of India 1978).

Paradoxically, this early experience did not strengthen the will to fortify and invigorate democratic institutions at the local level.[5] What it did was to buttress the faith in bureaucracy to implement development programmes (Mathur 2013). All the programmes that were initiated after 1966, like those promoting the Green Revolution or implementing anti-poverty programmes, such as Small and Marginal Farmers Agency and, ultimately, Integrated

---

[5] Constitutional amendment came only in 1993. Even this amendment has not helped in strengthening faith in people's participation in local-level governance. See Mathur (2006).

Rural Development Programme relied on the existing administrative system to implement them. So what has happened is that as the state began to expand its activities and initiate multiple development programmes, its capacity to administer and deliver public goods and services declined. But faith in this low-capacity administration to deliver them continued to remain high. The new agricultural strategy that delivered the Green Revolution further strengthened this belief and most programmes of development that were introduced after the failure of the Fourth Five-Year Plan were based on the bureaucratic strategy (Mathur 1982).

The bureaucratic strategy finds an echo in the education sector and was replicated in other social sectors too. In 1992–3, led by the World Bank, several multilateral agencies provided funds to expand and improve upon the quality of primary education. A large number of districts were chosen to implement what came to be known as District Primary Education Programme (DPEP). A separate bureaucratic structure, semi-autonomous of the existing one, was created with a top-down system providing guidelines, targets, and procedures. What emerged was a separate hierarchy where the civil servant with his transferable position had a much greater role to play than the educational expert, a primary school teacher, or a parent. The current programme of universalizing education follows the same route.

Thus, as the years went by and as the state expanded its development programmes, the dependence on the civil service, which was a successor to the earlier British one and which was alleged to have authoritarian features not in tune with the ethos of a developing country, grew at a fast pace. The civil service (IAS) acquired a pre-eminent role in Indian administration, occupying pivotal positions in the secretariat, field, and other agencies, governmental or semi-autonomous in nature, and became instrumental in taking most decisions about administrative performance and shaping it.

This near monopoly of all critical government positions and in other public institutions began to be questioned by many other functional services that were recruited in the same open manner of public recruitment. One of the first services to voice this concern of parity was the police service whose members headed the police administration at the district level. Invariably, the district collector from the IAS and the superintendent of police from the Indian Police Service (IPS) had difficulties in working together unless they could forge a personal equation. Another voice raised in this connection was that of the Indian Forest Service (IFS), another all-India service, which also had the forest officer posted at the district level. Other functional services, such as the Indian Audit and Accounts Service, Revenue Service and so on, began raising similar concerns for not reaching the levels of secretaries to the government. Inter-service rivalry increased as issues of pay parity and opportunities for advancement in career were raised.

The first ARC, as mentioned earlier, had recommended creation of functional domains in which after certain number of years of service the IAS could opt for a specialization. If accepted, this would have changed the character of the service and that of the administrative system. The second ARC while concluding that 'many of the recommendations involving basic changes have not be acted upon and therefore, the framework, systems and methods of functioning of the civil service based on the Whitehall model of nineteenth century remains largely unchanged' does not endorse any of these changes and only suggests pre-recruitment and post-recruitment procedural and institutional changes (Second Administrative Reforms Commission 2008: 23).

The issue of functional domains, pay parity, and career advancement continues to engender controversies around the IAS. Even as the new defence minister took over in 2017, a retired naval chief pointed out the acute shortage of expertise in military matters at the level of the secretariat, which is manned by the IAS. He laments that the fate of our military depends on civilian officers who run the ministry. He argues that these officers need to have domain knowledge for decisions to move quickly beyond file notings (Prakash 2017).

The Seventh Pay Commission that submitted its report towards the end of 2015 was also seized on this matter of pay parity and career opportunities and the edge that the IAS has in appointments to coveted administrative positions. The commission was unable to take a decision and was divided on this issue. The majority view in the commission was that as far as holding key positions in the central government is concerned, any officer with requisite experience should be eligible to apply for any senior post once he or she has cleared the screening. The chairman, while presenting the report to the finance minister, pointed out that the cause of grievance is that all posts covering the majority of domains today are manned by the IAS, be it technical or administrative. He further said that it is time that the government takes a call that being a subject expert and not a generalist should be the criterion to man a post. He further warned that the widening gap between the IAS and other services could lead to a chaotic situation. The member who gave a dissenting note said that it was not the pay panel's job to suggest changes that dilute the pivotal role of the IAS. Any review of the foundations of the 'steel frame' must be undertaken by a commission specially constituted for the purpose and not by a pay commission (Government of India 2015b: 185–93).[6]

Consequently, no decision in this regard was taken even when two of the three members of the commission supported the move towards dismantling the generalist orientation of the civil service. The Centre's decision to appoint a committee to process the recommendations of the Seventh Pay Commission overwhelmingly consisted of IAS officers. The Confederation of Civil Service Associations seemed to think that the fate of their demands was

---

[6] It may be noted that the dissenting voice was of an ex-IAS officer, a member of the commission.

already sealed with this kind of composition of the committee (*The Hindustan Times* 1 January 2016). Functional services deeply distrust the IAS in giving them fair treatment as far as personnel issues are concerned.[7]

Such a rivalry has created a dent in the image that the IAS had of itself. As per a survey conducted by the National Academy of Administration in 1995, the IAS 'thinks that they are intellectually of high calibre, committed to the organization, action and result focused, innovative and creative' (quoted in Bagchi 2007: 34). The Report of the Civil Services Review Committee (Alagh Committee) also conducted a survey of people's perceptions of the civil services and suggests that ordinary citizens lack accessibility to them.

A more stinging indictment has been made by the second ARC in its report on personnel administration. Bemoaning the fact that vast changes in the socio-political and economic fields that have taken place over the years have not led to attitudinal and behavioural change among the civil servants, it invokes Hegel to say that bureaucrats still think that exercise of power is a mission sanctioned by god. The report further adds that most of civil servants have been socialized to act in a manner that accentuates command and control methods rather than respond to people's needs and aspirations (Second Administrative Reforms Commission 2008: v). The IAS is facing huge challenges in not only living up to its own perceived image, but also using the mythology of yore to prop itself up.

The reason why the IAS has held public attention is because of the critical positions that it holds at all levels of government, whether of policymaking or implementation. The service also commands

---

[7] A confederation of civil service officers association met union minister and requested him to alter the composition of a high powered panel created recently to process the recommendations of the Seventh Pay Commission as they were apprehensive of their neutrality. Reported in *DNA*, 27 March 2016.

higher career opportunities and higher salary and perks. So its exercise of power irks other central services who then demand parity. Second, the issue has been of a generalist civil service becoming more influential than functionalist services who have knowledge and expertise in the domain. Lastly, there is frequent criticism of its elite nature and the ensuing behaviour. More indicting criticism has been of its generalist character. The first ARC recommended that the generalist civil service should move towards functional specialization and had categorized at least eight areas that the IAS officers could be groomed into. Critics continue to mention lack of knowledge of domain activity as the major weakness of the civil service. With increasing technological development, globalization, and digitization, domain knowledge is of utmost importance. In the final analysis, the IAS also carries the burdens of the past when state-led development programmes implemented through administrative agency have not yielded results.

The fact that the Constitution provides the IAS protection from undue political influence and gives it the capability to disagree with political masters has been a serious sore point in the relationship of the IAS with political leadership at all levels of government. While the service sees itself as a neutral, professional group of civil servants recruited on merit, politicians see it as instruments to implement legitimate public policies and even their instructions that may not be in public interest. This has led to many conflicts and different regimes have tended to resolve it in different ways.

3   Struggle for Political Control

The first serious assault on the nature of civil service and its role came from Prime Minister Indira Gandhi[1] and other leaders of the Congress party in 1969 in the form of their demand for a 'committed' civil service in contrast to a supposedly neutral one. The president of the Congress party in his address to a party convention suggested that the so-called neutral administrative machinery is an obstacle and not an aid in the pursuit of socialist goals. He argued that 'the present bureaucracy under the orthodox and conservative leadership of the ICS with its conservative upper class prejudices can hardly be expected to meet the requirements of social and economic change along socialist lines' (*Hindustan Times* December 1969).

A fierce debate followed in which retired and serving bureaucrats participated freely (Chaturvedi 1971; Dubhashi 1971; *Seminar* [Special Issue] 1973). The stand of Indira Gandhi and others was seen by the bureaucrats as an onslaught against the basic creed of their civil service and was bitterly opposed by them and their proponents. They labelled the move as a demand for personal loyalty

---

[1] Writing to a friend in 1966 after she had just taken over as prime minister, Indira Gandhi said 'the inertia of our civil service is incredible' and added 'we have a system of deadwood replacing deadwood' (quoted in Guha 2007: 499).

that would only lead to the politicization of civil service. Free and fearless advice to the political masters could not then be elicited from the civil servants and arbitrary actions would ensue.[2]

However, the Shah Commission, which was enjoined to investigate the excesses of the Emergency imposed by Gandhi in 1975,[3] pointed out that most IAS officers in secretariats and districts accepted orders that they believed were improper and politically motivated. There were many cases where 'officers curried favour with politicians by doing what they thought people in authority desired'. By the time the Emergency ended, political colonization of the civil service was complete (Das 1998: 148). Even the IAS officers themselves believed that the service had changed irrevocably during the period. Many civil servants writing in newspapers reiterated that the role of civil service had changed drastically and professionalism was giving place to loyalty. Anand Sarup, a retired civil servant, writing in the *Times of India* (6 January 1990), said that bureaucrats had learned to adjust to the compulsions of politicians. In fact, the more enterprising among them have learned to anticipate the wishes of their political masters and to deliver unasked whatever is necessary for their personal or political welfare. Such bureaucrats earn a reputation and get ahead in their career. Sometime earlier, a civil servant writing in 1983 pointed out that 'newly elected ministers usually wanted to do certain things—possibly in fulfillment of electoral promises given generously rather than wisely'. As the proportion of less experienced ministers increases, the more is their ministerial

---

[2] In this demand they got support from what Sardar Patel had spoken about in the Constituent Assembly while defending the role of the civil services: 'If you want an efficient All-India Service advise you to allow the services to open their mouths freely ... allow them to express their opinions without fear or favour'.

[3] Chaired by Justice J.C. Shah, a retired chief justice of India, the Shah Commission of Inquiry was appointed by the Government of India in 1977.

preference for administrators who support their line of action without raising uncomfortable questions or doubts (Potter 1986: 158).

The government did not pursue the issue of neutrality versus commitment. No formal change took place but the practice of shifting bureaucrats on demands of political leadership began a tendency that is widespread in the system today. The period of the Emergency, when loyalty became an important criterion for holding a pivotal position in government, was replicated by the Janata Party when it came to power by defeating the Congress and Indira Gandhi. The return of the Congress and defeat of the Janata Party in 1980 signalled the repeat of emphasis on loyalty. The practice has spawned what is colloquially known as 'transfer industry', permeating both the central as well as the state governments (Banik 2001; Das 1998; Potter 1986). Formal acceptance of this idea would have transformed the role and structure of the civil service and the process of its recruitment but this did not happen. What could not be formalized was openly accepted in practice.[4]

Before Independence, transfers served several purposes in moulding the traditions of the British colonial service. Foremost, transfers were the most important method of creating a generalist civil service. Bright young men with specializations in any subject—ranging from linguists to botany to economics—were chosen through a competitive examination. What was judged was the quality of their intellect and not their knowledge of a particular subject. Having had this characteristic assured through the recruitment process, the first step was to allow the civil servant to move from one post to another while technical officers remained in their

[4] It must be emphasized, however, that all transfers are not only due to political choices to create a loyal team. Transfers can occur due to natural reasons such as leave, retirement, and so on and can also take place on the request of civil servants themselves for personal reasons. Transfers are also inherent in the generalist civil service where advances in career take place by acquiring experience of administering diverse fields.

subordinate offices or departments. The whole structure of the Raj celebrated generalist control and continuity, not specialist expertise and innovation (Potter 1986: 34). Transfers were often too quick to be liked by the individuals, but were accepted for they were assumed to fulfill a particular purpose.

Transfers served two other purposes for the colonial administration. One was to avoid excessive 'embeddedness' in local society by creating some distance between the civil servants and local society (Banik 2007: 107). This was also intended to reduce the influence of caste and family relationships or friendships detrimental to the functional duties. The other purpose was to acquaint the British recruits with the diversity of life, complexities of culture, and difficulties of terrain in India.[5]

When market reforms were initiated in 1991, public administration in India reflected characteristics of an inherited colonial administration with the pathologies of a Weberian hierarchical model. The working of the democracy and the interaction with the socio-political system brought in features that made a mockery of both—an ideal British inheritance and an ideal classical practice. Individual bureaucrats became pillars of whatever success was achieved in running specific government programmes, and political leadership relied on these chosen officers to deliver results that they cherished. Political leadership tended to fill in crucial command and control positions in the governmental system through personal appointees. Thus, without systemic change, a patronage system evolved keeping the charade of neutral, impartial bureaucracy.

Another significant development took place. Prime ministers increasingly relied on their chosen bureaucrats as advisors and

---

[5] It has been reported that in 2007 the UPA government attempted to enforce the norm of a 'three-year tenure'. This was an effort to ensure continuity in a job for purposes of performance evaluation and accountability.

implementers of public policy. The traditional administrative structure that had the cabinet secretariat with a cabinet secretary as its head declined in its influence and role. The prime minister's secretariat began to displace it. This ascendancy was gradual, with the prime minister's secretariat during the time of Indira Gandhi attaining a pre-eminent role. The practice has been followed by later prime ministers, and the current prime minister, Narendra Modi, is alleged to have centralized power through this mechanism. This practice has resulted in further empowering the bureaucrats who man this secretariat (Mookerjee 2018).

Many civil servants themselves became critical of the public administration that they served and their lack of achievements became the staple of public discourse. A senior member of the IAS, who was an additional secretary in the Department of Administrative Reforms, Government of India, writing for the special number of the *Indian Journal of Public Administration* entitled 'Fifty Years of Indian Administration: Retrospect and Prospect' (1997: 554) concluded that 'public administration and civil services appear to be passing through difficult times in terms of eroded credibility and effectiveness of the civil service, growing public perceptions of an unholy nexus between politicians, civil servants and criminals, and an increasing criticism of the low level of honesty, transparency and accessibility of the democratic elements in charge of administration'. This sentiment was echoed by another civil servant writing in the same journal in its special issue 'Excellence in Public Service' in 2006 (Dhar 2006: 451).

What is puzzling is that the government also voiced these concerns in its various reports, and each prime minister, usually in their first year in office, made scathing criticism of the administration they were heading. The Twelfth Five-Year Plan (2012–17) carried on the tradition of earlier plans, lamenting the weaknesses in the implementation processes and emphasizing that 'implementation is the key' (xv). The Second Administrative Reforms Commission mentioned in its report that there has been no sincere attempt to restructure the civil service, although more than 600 committees and commissions have looked at different aspects of public administration in the country Responding to the comment of a distinguished scholar that India's efforts at reform 'amounted to correction slips to the inherited administrative system', the commission went on to say that they were not even correction slips but were more in the nature of endorsement slips (Second Administrative Reforms Commission 2008: 3).

Successive prime ministers have expressed similar concerns when they have assumed office. Nehru has already been mentioned above. Assuming the highest office, Indira Gandhi said in 1966 that what India needed today was a 'revolution in administrative system', and declared a year later that 'if a large proportion of the investment we have made under the plans remains unutilized, the cause is to be found in administrative shortcomings'. Rajiv Gandhi was more blunt and forthright when in a speech in Bombay he said: 'We have government servants who do not serve but oppress the poor, they have no work ethics, no feeling for public cause, no involvement in the future of the nation' (quoted in Mathur 2014: 198). A.B. Vajpayee, addressing the National Development Council in 1999, voiced similar sentiments when he said that 'people often perceive the bureaucracy as an agent of exploitation rather than provider of service. Corruption has become low risk high reward activity' (Mathur 2014: 198). Prime Minister Manmohan Singh, on assuming office in 2004, complained: 'I am convinced that government at every level, is not adequately equipped and attuned to deal with it (social and economic change) and meet the aspirations of the people. To be able to do so we require the reform of government and of public institutions' (quoted in Mathur 2005: 56). Possibly, it was this comment that led to appointment of the Second Administrative Reforms Commission by his government in 2005.

The newly elected prime minister, Narendra Modi (2014), has an entirely different approach towards bureaucracy. He has not

commented on its failings and has sought its support in implementing his developmental agenda. In a meeting with 77 top bureaucrats
(secretaries to Government of India), the prime minister expressed
'full faith in their commitment and competence to build a better
future of the country' (*Times of India* 4 June 2014). He exhorted them
to take decisions without fear or favour while continuing the practice
of appointing chosen bureaucrats to critical positions in government.
He also encouraged them to have direct links with his office and not
necessarily through the minister who headed their ministries.[6]

In keeping with this overture, the prime minister now keeps
himself in direct touch with civil servants in states and central ministries through monthly meetings conducted via teleconferencing.
He reviews projects and gives directions to remove obstacles, reduce
red tape, or improve coordination. The ministers in charge of the
relevant portfolios are kept out of these meetings. This monitoring platform has been named Proactive Governance and Timely
Implementation (PRAGATI). Projects are treated on a case-by-
case-basis and no effort is made for systemic change. It is this process of interacting directly with senior members of civil service and
empowering the Prime Minister's Office that has led to the charge
of centralization of powers by the prime minister.[7]

---

[6] It has been estimated that in over 16 months since Modi government
came to power in 2014, 80 secretaries to Government of India have been
reshuffled. This reshuffling has taken place at the behest of Prime Minister's Office not of individual Ministers. See A.K. Bhattacharya (2015).

[7] Commenting in *Business Standard* (8 February 2016), Bhattacharya
contends that after 20 months in power, Prime Minister Modi looks different from other prime ministers in his engagement with bureaucracy. He
has established direct contact with senior bureaucrats, bypassing their ministers, and monitors performance of key projects. Transfers take place more
on the ability to deliver. Unlike previous incumbents, Modi has made no
pretence or promise of reforming the bureaucracy.

The Prime Minister's Office is no more an office providing sec-
retarial assistance to the prime minister. It now functions through
25 sections that monitor policy and its implementation by all ministries. The latest example of how it functions was demonstrated
when it stepped in to withdraw guidelines regarding fake news by
the Information and Broadcasting Ministry.[8]

The Modi-led government is making an effort to change the
orientation of bureaucracy, which had earlier worked in an environment of state-directed and controlled development and now
had to support business that had become the lead player and thus
encourage private investment. Direct interaction with civil servants
and allowing them to publicly express policy concerns and trusting
them are ways that are being adopted.

Modi apparently places tremendous faith in the civil service and
its multifaceted competence. He reflects the belief that well-trained,
intelligent generalists can effectively discharge any responsibility
assigned to them.

This mode of extending bureaucratic support resonates with the
way the federal system is transforming itself in the face of globalization and liberalization. States are being encouraged to compete
for private investment and to pursue their projects. Chief ministers with their bureaucratic advisers are travelling abroad, seeking
opportunities for trade and business and soliciting multinationals
and non-resident Indians to invest in their states. This has greatly
diluted the demand of states on Centre for more funds and, at the
same time, has given greater freedom to states to use their own
strategies to raise funds.

In devising their own strategies for an improved business environment, states are demanding that their bureaucracies become

---

[8] Based on information received through RTI Act, Mookerji (*Business
Standard* 5 April 2018) provides a detailed description of the structure and
functions of the Prime Minister's Office.

receptive to business demands and flexible for change. The focus of their concern is not so much the structure of the administrative system but the attitudes of bureaucracy towards business and making administrative process friendlier for facilitating what the World Bank calls 'ease of doing business'. A pro-business impetus was the central theme of a former chief minister of Andhra Pradesh when he mentioned in his autobiography, 'When I started interacting directly with industry, they would tell me: your officials look down upon industry; they treat us as starting points of all ills in society' (quoted in Murali 2017: 90–1).

This changed environment has put greater pressure on the administrative system to transform itself into playing a facilitative role of creating favourable business climate.

However, some state bureaucracies respond to these overtures more easily as compared to other states (Sinha 2005). Gujarat did not have much difficulty in responding to a liberal regime. As Sinha (2005: 91) points out, its bureaucracy was strongly supportive of the private sector even in the License Raj. This was not the case with the West Bengal bureaucracy. With the Gujarat development experience coming up prominently in public discourse after Modi became prime minister, the business-friendly attitude of the state's bureaucracy is being held as a model to be emulated. The lesson to be learnt was that it was possible to achieve development goals with the conventional administrative system through partnership with bureaucracy.

Let me also conclude by underlining the fact that bureaucrats and technocrats as individuals have been relied upon by prime ministers frequently to implement their programmes and policies, whatever their public stance on administrative reforms may have been. In turn, the bureaucratic elite has been supportive of prime ministers perceived to be strong willed and decisive. We have already referred to Nehru's reliance on the civil service. Raghavan (2014) contends that Indira Gandhi in 1970, facing difficult political situation and isolation from the then leadership of the Congress party, resorted to increasing centralization and vesting powers in trusted bureaucrats and technocrats as opposed to elected officials. He further suggests that the bureaucratic elite was most receptive to the Emergency. In fact, he quotes B.K. Nehru advising Indira Gandhi to take advantage of the Emergency imposed in 1975 to install a strong executive at the Centre capable of taking tough, unpleasant, and unpopular decisions (Raghavan 2014: 225). Prime Minister Modi is an exemplar in this regard. He has institutionalized his relationship with top bureaucrats to bypass the political leadership in his party.

Thus, the irony is that while the prime ministers generally express dissatisfaction with the administrative system when they assume office, they freely rely on the bureaucratic elite to pursue their policies and programmes.

To sum up, it appears that the government in India has found itself in a quandary as far as administrative reforms are concerned. As the story of Nehru's engagement with Paul Appleby's reports shows, personal efforts of even the prime minister could not achieve results. The colonial ways of governance became even more entrenched as time went on, and the efforts at reform sought to strengthen the very instrument that the reformers wanted to blunt. Writing in 2007 (448), Chandavarkar laid emphasis on the fact that 'government was described by the officials as an entity that stood aloof from society. Its relationship with its subjects continued to be conducted in the language of supplication and concession, demands and grants, charters and petitions, grievances and repression. At the same time, it appropriated greater executive powers'.

The predominant role ascribed to the IAS, like its predecessor in earlier times, got reinforced. Governments still needed to implement their programmes and policies; loyalty and reliability also became the required attributes of a civil servant. Neutrality and anonymity became victims in this process. Consequently, the government strategy changed. Political leaders began to bend the system rather than break it. They made bureaucrats partners in their endeavours. This partnership has had an enduring impact on Indian administration, yielding mixed results. Such partnership changed the relationship between the politicians and the civil servants, though. While the aim of the partnership was to draw on the political feasibility of the politicians' resources and the technological resources of civil servants, too often it led both partners to the pursuit of political or personal goals which did not serve public interest. It is this malaise that has attracted concerns about the decline of administration in India and concern about administrative reform.

4 The Formal Reform Effort

We have pointed out that the first prime minister considered his inability to reform public administration as his failing. Most of the successive prime ministers, while expressing incompatibility of administration with emerging demands of development, have sought support from the civil service to carry on their agenda. Formal efforts were made in this regard but little effective change took place. The political concerns for reforms reflected the context in which they were made. Also, the narrative shows that governments have not shown any hesitation in appointing committees and commissions for recommending reforms but have shown little inclination in implementing them. These appointments have served the political purpose of creating a perception of reform initiation; however, the governments have used the administration for their own purposes.

As pointed out earlier, the initial assessment of administration laid emphasis on the schism between the old and the new systems, pointing out that development could not be achieved by the inherited colonial administration. This view gained scholarly attention really after Paul Appleby was invited by the Government of India to report on Indian administration. He expressed the view that there was a dichotomy between bureaucratic dispositions and development needs in India (Appleby 1953). Some Ford Foundation experts reinforced this view when they recalled their work in community development programmes and commented that '… the inadequacies of the Indian bureaucracy are not due to the fact that it is bureaucracy but due to considerable fact that it carries too much baggage from the past' (Taylor et al. 1966: 579). This view gained further support when scholars such as LaPalombara (1963: 1) wrote, 'Public Administration steeped in the tradition of the Indian Civil Service may be less useful as developmental administrators than those who are not so rigidly tied to the notions of bureaucratic status, hierarchy and impartiality.'

The report of Paul Appleby was important not only for its contribution in setting up the Indian Institute of Public Administration and establishing Organization and Methods divisions in government ministries for continuous reform effort, but also in opening up Indian administrators and reformers to the ideas of development administration that were emerging as a way of viewing administrative reform in developing countries.

Paul Appleby's report is important also from another point of view. India's first prime minister, Jawaharlal Nehru, took deep personal interest in his work. Through the medium of his fortnightly letters to the chief ministers, Nehru constantly shared his views on the report in general and aspects of administration in particular.[1] As Saxena (2004: 169) points out, 'It is truly remarkable how such an incredibly busy person could underline the administrative problems again and again for the attention of his colleagues.' This frequent reference to Paul Appleby's report and discussion in the Parliament gave credence to his analysis of administrative problems and ways to resolve them. Nehru's confession of his failure to change Indian administration, quoted earlier, underlines the hurdles to bring about reform even when it was promoted by the highest executive of the

---

[1] So long as he was prime minister, Jawaharlal Nehru continued to preside over the annual meetings of Indian Institute of Public Administration and give his presidential address.

country. This was the only administrative reform report that was discussed in the Parliament and the prime minister chose to reply to the debate (Saxena 2004).

What is important to note is that after the Appleby Report of 1953, till 1966 no other expert or committee was appointed to have a broad look at administration. Even though Paul Appleby (1953: 54) had commented that Indian personnel administration 'has too much feudalistic heritage, too much academic and "intellectuality" orientation, too little administrative action and human-relations orientation, and is too defensive of the "rights" of existing personnel', he induced some kind of self-pride and smugness among the reformers when he also emphasized in his report that Government of India could be rated among the dozen or so well-administered countries of the world.[2] He discounted some of the popular criticisms of administration as blanket indictments and then went on to say that 'India is among dozen or so governments in which honesty has been carried to its highest levels'. As Braibanti (1966: 145) says, Appleby concluded his remarks in 'a language of delicacy and finesse' and saw his report widely distributed with the finance minister claiming with some pride that it was he who brought Appleby to India. Armed with many certificates of this kind, the government initiated few administrative reform activities till the end of the Third Five-Year Plan, which was also the time when the postponement of the Fourth Five-Year Plan was announced in 1966.

Appleby laid emphasis on professionalization of the civil service and continuous interaction with academics for reform. He thought that the establishment of Indian Institute of Public Administration, a recommendation that was readily accepted, would facilitate this process. As a matter of fact, the institute did seek to set the agenda that was to shape the study and practice of public administration in

[2] This remark is in capital letters in the report and was widely quoted at that time.

India.[3] One significant effort that the institute undertook in this direction was to establish a graduate programme in the study of public administration in which a number of university academics were exposed to largely American disciplinary developments in the field. A number of these academics went back to universities to begin similar graduate programmes of study, thus rapidly diffusing American ideas of professional public administration. A separate field of study, development administration, was already emerging as an important dimension of American aid efforts and was soon to become major intellectual export to developing countries.

In transmitting the doctrine and practice of public administration from United States to India, Ford Foundation, apart from US Agency for International Development and the United Nations, played a major role (Braibanti 1966). Paul Appleby's trip was sponsored through the auspices of the Ford Foundation, which alone spent US$ 360,400 in grants to institutions and US$ 76,000 in providing consultants and specialists to improve public administration in India during 1951–62 (Braibanti 1966: 148). An important consequence of this financial and technical aid, as well as the intellectual thrust of administration they promoted, was that it began to be believed that change in the colonial administrative system can be brought about by changing the behaviour and the professional capacity of the individual bureaucrat. This was possible through education and training programmes. Training institutions proliferated and studies that supported this broad argument multiplied. Large number of scholars were attracted to the field of development administration, motivated not only by scholarly reasons, but also by the belief that administration was the instrument of change and that administrative behaviour could be transformed without structural changes in the colonial administrative structure and procedure.

[3] On the occasion of the 50th year of its establishment, the institute decided to bring out a publication in the memory of Paul Appleby. See Reddy et al. (2004).

ADMINISTRATIVE REFORMS COMMISSION, 1966–70, AND ITS IMPACT

After the submission of the Appleby Report in 1953, few significant government efforts were made to reform the administration even though some important initiatives were undertaken in the field of rural development. With the acknowledgement of Plan failures and announcement of Plan holiday, attention once again turned towards reforming public administration. Nehru had been succeeded by Lal Bahadur Shastri, who announced the appointment of the Administrative Reforms Commission in 1966, patterned after Hoover Commission of the US, having a political and civil servant membership with experts coming in to write reports after study and research. He appointed a political rival of his as chairman of the commission, who soon resigned to take part in active politics. His successor in the commission did not command a high political stature. The commission worked over a period of 4 years making a total of 581 recommendations (Maheshwari 1993: 116). The commission made little impact for no recommendation of consequence was accepted.

However, it was not as if recommendations of consequence were not made. As Jain (2000: 210) points out, the acceptance of the suggestion that many existing civil services should be regrouped into eight functional categories, with the IAS becoming a generalist service having functional role of revenue administration, would have changed the entire character of Indian administration. It would have led to the creation of an expert/specialist system of administration and weakened the 'steel frame' inherited from the British and alleged to be the main component of colonial legacy.

The politicians who became members of the commission did not command prestige and influence with the government of the day and had little influence with the government. As a matter of fact, the government itself was in a flux. Lal Bahadur Shastri, the prime minister who had appointed the commission, suddenly died soon after and

Indira Gandhi took over. For the years up to 1971 she was fighting for her political survival, attending to crises, and did not find time to reflect on administrative change. When the commission finished its tasks, the country was facing a war for the liberation of Bangladesh and was subsequently caught in the turmoil of national Emergency. The ruling party was comfortable working with the existing administrative system, and reforming it was not on the agenda of the political parties in opposition. The Administrative Reforms Commission just faded away, leaving behind a pile of reports and frustration at the national inability to reform a colonial administrative system.

But the legacy of reform efforts of the commission and earlier transnational commentaries lingered. The academic researchers took it upon themselves to pose the question of whether the traditional bureaucratic structure and behavioural norms were at all compatible with the new task of administering development. Several studies followed.[4] These studies, based on empirical attitudinal surveys, attempted to present behavioural profiles of administrators and show that these did not match with the expected profiles of those involved in development tasks. The studies assumed that the performance of the administrators was dependent on their mental make-up and a 'developmentalist' was needed to implement development policies.

With rural development and removal of poverty being high on the policy agenda, another significant strand of research highlighting the relationship with politicians and administrators emerged. It was argued that the success of local democratic institutions in promoting development rested on the ability of the political and administrative leadership to cooperate with one another and resolve the tensions and conflicts emerging from social environment.[5] What is

[4] For example, see Mathur (1972a and 1972b); Panandiker and Kshirsagar (1978); and Bhambhri (1972).

[5] See, for example, Kothari and Roy (1969); Gaikwad (1969); Bjorkman (1976); and Chaturvedi (1964).

significant is that these kinds of studies that gained in popularity among many scholars emerging from the shadow of comments of early national and American scholars looked at bureaucratic behaviour as a product of interpersonal relationships and group dynamics occurring within specific organizational boundaries. The role of bureaucratic structure and processes in influencing behaviour began to recede from the agenda of reform and attention began to be focused on changing behavioural orientations.

Little concern for administrative reform that would bring about change in traditional administrative system was expressed in the 1970s and later. The decade of 1970s was marked by a war, declaration of the Emergency signalling the suspension of democratic processes, emergence of a government led by a motley crowd of political parties opposed to Congress party that had declared Emergency, and then political instability. The Opposition parties that came to power after the defeat of the Congress party and after the Emergency appointed a commission to enquire into the excesses committed during the Emergency period. The commission headed by a retired judge of the Supreme Court made severe indictment of the civil service and reported that it carried out instructions from politicians and administrative heads on personal and political considerations. There were many cases where officers curried favour with politicians by doing what they thought the people in authority desired. In short, the evidence showed, as a journalist remarked, '[The Emergency was] the high water-mark of the politicians' victory in the long drawn out struggle against the civil service' (quoted in Potter 1986: 157). But this was also an opening for those bureaucrats who used the system for their personal benefit. Corruption became an endemic feature of India's administration and gained strength as the bureaucrats and politicians found the system mutually rewarding. No wonder there was little interest in administrative reform (Das 2001).

The Government of India went on to appoint the Second Reforms Commission in 2005, nearly 40 years after the first had been appointed. It carried the mandate that 'the Commission will suggest measures to achieve a proactive, responsive, accountable, sustainable and efficient administration for the country at all levels of the government'. It submitted around 15 reports: the first one in 2006 and last one in 2009. The process of consideration of these reports had hardly begun when elections were called, and though the same political coalition came back to power, the concern for administrative reforms did not figure high on the agenda. This was also the period when faith in the market to deliver public goods and services was on ascendance and the government began to show its keenness in designing institutions that will incorporate the private sector and its practices.

The commissions were not the only sources that provided a plethora of recommendations to reform public administration in India. Another source has been the Plan documents.

The Eighth Five-Year Plan (1992–7) began to set the context for the change necessary for the government to adopt neoliberal policies. Reflecting global processes, the Plan recognized that all over the world, centralized economies are disintegrating. On the other hand, economies of several regions are getting integrated under a common philosophy of growth guided by market forces and liberal policies. The emphasis is on autonomy and efficiency and liberal policies.

It added that the role of the state is to provide an environment in which market friendly institutions can grow and sustain themselves, and made a plea to support the voluntary sector to grow with market forces. Pointing out that the Plan will have to undertake re-examination and re-orientation of the role of government, it went on to underline two further issues. First, it set the stage for closing down of public sector units making losses and recommended that the rationale of public sector entering certain industrial areas needs to be re-examined. Second, the Plan saw it necessary to make development a people's movement. A lot in the areas of education, health, and land improvement can be accomplished by creating people's institutions that are accountable to the community.

This was the first Plan document that came after the dismantling of the planning regime which reflected some of the tenets of new public management and began to lay emphasis on efficiency and economy in government performance. It wanted the scope of the public sector to be reduced and that of the private sector expanded by involving civil society organizations in implementing many tasks in the social sector.

Subsequent five-year plans continued to endorse the message of creating an environment that provided support to market forces, free competition, and role of the voluntary sector. The Eleventh Five-Year Plan emphasized improvement in governance to launch these initiatives. It mentioned that 'experience suggests that many of these initiatives have floundered because of poor design, insufficient accountability and also corruption at various levels'.

The Twelfth Five-Year Plan carried the same message while endorsing the recommendations of the Second Administrative Reforms Commission. It laid considerable emphasis on social mobilization and the role of the voluntary sector and civil society in achieving Plan objectives. The significance of these recommendations of Plan documents lies in the period in which they were written in. Liberal economic policies had been introduced even though planning had not been replaced yet. This was a departure from the exhortations of the earlier plans that had laid emphasis on strengthening the administrative system for a state-led development.

Thus, with the adoption of liberal policies, India also began to focus on the issues of good governance. In 1992 itself the plea to change the role of state and its orientation began to take shape. Transparency and accountability began to emerge as key issues for improved implementation of development programmes.

Another source of recommendations for reform has been of the pay commissions that came during the liberal period. The first full-fledged recommendation that reflected the neoliberal perspective of administration and reform came with the recommendations of the Fifth Pay Commission. This commission was set up in 1994 by the Government of India and submitted its report in 1997. Though its main task was to suggest changes in the pay and allowances and related conditions of central government servants, an additional charge was given to it. To the usual terms of reference of a pay commission, the government added a new one. This was to include suggestions for linking enhancement of pay and allowances to performance. It demonstrated that the government was also interested in relating enhancement of employees' working and salary conditions with greater contribution to efficiency. The link between enhancement of pay and allowances and performance was emphasized by the commission when it did not accept the argument of staff associations that such recommendations be separated from those for pay and allowances and presented in a separate report. The commission's stand was 'that there is an inextricable link between the quality and quantity of manpower, the resultant quality, utility and cost effectiveness of public administration and the corresponding compensation package. The pay scale and allowances cannot be simply determined without reference to the organization and size of the Government machinery' (Government of India 1996: para 2.3).[6]

The global perspective of administrative reform emerging from new public management was also echoed in the manner in which the Pay Commission gathered knowledge and framed its recommendations. The commission resorted to consultancies from private sector specialists and also visited several Commonwealth countries where such reforms had been undertaken. It drew several lessons from this experience of visiting other countries which

---

[6] Notation refers to chapter number and number of the paragraph in the Pay Commission report. This has been taken from Appendix I in Mehta (2000: 223–444).

suggested to it that, among other things, rightsizing of the government and reducing its flab, privatization of many of its functions through corporatization or contracting it and defining core duties of the government were important dimensions of reforms that had been undertaken elsewhere.

Some of the recommendations have had direct impact on the thinking about the existing administrative system without actually reforming it. The commission provided a neoliberal perspective on administrative reforms that has influenced the governments that came after it. Though its recommendations were not explicitly accepted, they have, however, given successive governments a broad direction and path to follow. In recommending reforms in India, donor agencies and international consultants frequently referred to successful experiences that had followed the new public management perspective in other countries. The easy acceptance of this perspective of reforms among the policy planners was partly due to the failure of reforming the administration inherited from the British colonial times. We have already shown that numerous reports and recommendations did not do much to trigger reform and many pathologies in the system were actually accepted as an ongoing part of the administrative system. Thus, privatization or shedding functions or creating a new institutional structure for contracted-out services was a comparatively easy way out, rather than moving an elephant in the room.

The Fifth Pay Commission laid out its perspective for changes in pay and allowances by enumerating core functions of the government and what it should not do. It suggested that the following should be included in the legitimate province of the government: (*i*) security, (*ii*) international relations, (*iii*) law and order, (*iv*) management of economy at the national level, (*v*) setting up of infrastructure, (*vi*) social services, and (*vii*) programmes for disadvantaged sections. Then, it dissuaded the government from participating directly in manufacturing, mining, and economic services and from directly controlling private activity in the economic sphere. Disinvestment was also part of the recommendations made by the commission. It further mentioned that in cases where certain economic activities have been retained by the government, they have been hived off into separate autonomous agencies that function independently (Government of India 1996: para 4.6). In the next para, the Pay Commission says that government should not insist on issuing licenses and permits for setting up economic activities. 'It is considered wiser to set up autonomous regulating agencies with quasi-judicial powers, in order to ensure that the functioning of private units is regulated in social interest.'

In the immediate aftermath of the presentation of the Fifth Pay Commission report, while the government and the staff associations grappled with issues arising out of recommendations on rationalization of pay and allowances, rightsizing the government was a subject of some public discussion. It was widely believed that the Indian bureaucracy was obese and flabby, leading to high degrees of inefficiencies. Communication channels became unduly long, which led to delays and diffusion of responsibility. So the first effort at reform needed to slim down this bureaucracy. The Fifth Pay Commission had argued that 'no doubt that work had expanded [since 1948], but the expansion of the government is disproportionate to the increase of workload'. It recommended that over a period of 10 years, the staff strength had to be reduced by 30 per cent and a large number of vacant posts need to be abolished.

The formal reforms commissions, pay commissions, and the Plans have provided a plethora of recommendations. It is now widely acknowledged that these have made little dent on the inherited system. The Second Reforms Commission itself has mentioned that no significant change has taken place and was constrained to remark that the administration continues to tread the nineteenth-century colonial path.

5   Western Influence

Neoliberal Perspectives for Reforming Administration

Even though colonial practices have entrenched themselves and the political establishment has found its own ways to go around them to achieve its goals, administration has not remained the same. Silent changes have begun to appear in the last two decades.

As neoliberalism begins to unfold its charm in the academic world and practitioners begin to find its agenda as a useful armoury to respond to the problems of delivering public goods and services, it will be good to remind ourselves of a high fashion of earlier years that made a deep impact on the study and practice of public administration in India. When international assistance for development began on a large scale in the 1950s, it was realized that many of the recipient states did not have the capability to utilize the aid that was being given to them. Strengthening state capability through empowerment of bureaucracy became high on the agenda of aid-giving agencies. If today's concern about governance is emanating from international financial institutions such as the World Bank and International Monetary Fund (IMF), at that time it was being expressed by agencies such as the Ford Foundation and United Nations Development Programme (UNDP). That concern generated an academic industry of its own and what came to be known as development administration movement took shape.

Development administration demarcated itself as a separate field of study and practice. One of the earliest users of the term argued that its aim was to specify the focus of administration on support and management of development as distinguished from law and order and revenue collection. He went on to claim that 'the function of development administration is to assure that an appropriately congenial environment and effective administrative support is provided for delivery of capital, materials and services where needed in the productive process—whether in public, private or mixed economies' (Gant 1979: 20). While the term seems to have been coined earlier, the prime mover in conceptualizing the field was the Comparative Administration Group (CAG) led by Fred Riggs. Financially supported by the Ford Foundation, CAG sponsored research, conducted seminars, and published books and monographs on the experience of developing countries. Much of this history has been documented extensively by Riggs himself while reviewing the work of CAG (Riggs 1976). The point is that during the decades of the 1960s and 1970s, which were also known as development decades, development administration had an unprecedented influence in shaping academic agendas of university departments and influencing the policies of international donor agencies such as the UNDP and the Ford Foundation.

The broad perspective of development administration was that of a technically oriented, professionally competent, and politically and ideologically neutral bureaucracy. Such a bureaucracy was seen as a mirror image of bureaucracies in the Western world. Thus, a related belief was that institutional imitation was bound to produce results similar to those obtained in the developed world: efficiency, increased rationality and the like at a very general level. The more developed (that is, bureaucratic and Western like) an administrative system became, the greater the likelihood that it would have developmental effects (Dwivedi and Henderson 1990:13).

The strategy proposed to bring about this kind of reform was to impart extensive training to civil servants. While structural and procedural changes were not ruled out, it was expected that training would create such awareness among the bureaucrats that they will themselves design these changes without external suggestions. In a United Nations document (1975: 87) that succinctly summarized the direction its programme on public administration was taking, training found an important place.

After an experience of nearly two decades, disillusionment with the whole concept of development administration and its intended focus to bring about reform in the developing countries set in. The proliferation of scholarly contributions was not sufficient in getting ideas of reform implemented. What began to be questioned was the nature of knowledge and the framework used to generate it. The emphasis on professional attributes and using training to impart them to bureaucracy induced public administration to become inward looking. Strengthening bureaucracy opened vistas for mis-use of its role where other social groups were weak, providing no or little countervailing force. Its insulation made it unresponsive to the needs of society. The influence of CAG, which had become a star on the academic firmament, began to fade in the 1970s and it lost its financial support from the Ford Foundation soon after.

The experience of development also made it evident that the task of nation-building and the goals of development were issues of keen contestation in the concerned countries. There were social groups that mobilized power to design development programmes and strategies in such a way that they stood to benefit from them. The actual design of development emerged from political compro-mises and bargains. Such compromises and bargains were not always in larger public interest. In such a situation, bureaucracy could not possibly play a neutral role. Riggs and many of his colleagues began to argue that the imbalance in the power equations of political and administrative systems was not conducive to the development of democracy in developing countries (see in particular Riggs 1965).

In a further indictment of development administration, Riggs (1998) questioned the assumption that bureaucracies could be essentially non-political instruments of public policy, thought that separation of politics and administration was a myth, and also questioned the belief that bad practices were due to ignorance and that knowledge of better practices would lead folks anywhere to adopt them. Significantly he went on to say, 'We did not question what worked in America would also work in other countries, nor did we suppose that people in other countries may have good reasons of doing what they did or that there were people with vested interests in the status quo who would resist changes that might infringe on their privileges' (Riggs 1998: 24).

What is significant in these assessments was the realization that reform and change are not value-neutral terms. This self-evaluation coming from a leading exponent of the development administration movement holds many lessons for us who are now grappling with new fashion of governance reforms. A grand project that involved a large number of intellectuals who spawned aid-giving agencies, creating training institutions that brought together thousands of administrators and giving a different slant to the study of public administration, came to grief because public administration was seen in a sanitized way. It was not seen as a product of political contestation and negotiation. We seem to be forgetting this lesson as we grapple with governance reforms. More of this shall be discussed later.

RISE OF NEOLIBERALISM

Public administration in the developed countries was facing other challenges, which called for different types of reforms or corrections. This was prompted by the ascendance of liberalization and market reforms. What began as government enterprises, such as airlines, electricity, telecommunications, were now being sought to be privatized. Infrastructure for increasing growth was in shambles and government was reaching out to the private sector for finances and technology to improve and build it. In this environment, quality of basic governmental functions began to be questioned and the slogan that emerged was 'less of government and more of market'. It was generally agreed, as Roberts (2010: 4) points out, that the primary goal of the public sector was to have less of it, and the critical tactical question was how government can make an orderly retreat by trimming its now redundant appendages.

The liberalization–globalization package of policies had at least one important consequence, among many others. One was that the perspective on the role of state and conceptualization of governance began to change. The state began to be seen as a problem rather than as a solution to many of the economic problems that many countries in the developed world were facing. The slogan 'less government and more governance' began to catch the imagination of people. In this conceptualization, the private sector gained salience in the public domain as an important actor with the state delivering public goods and services.

NEW PUBLIC MANAGEMENT AND ITS CONCEPTUAL ASSUMPTIONS

Faith in the market led to scholarly focus on managerial practices in the private sector, which, in turn, led to higher performance and efficiency. Economists began to ask what sorts of behaviour would be expected if individuals in the public sector—politicians and bureaucrats—were seen to behave as individuals in the marketplace, where it was assumed that they pursue their self-interests as rational utility-maximizers. Using economic tools to understand the behaviour of individuals in the public sector, economists of this persuasion gave birth to what has come to be known as public choice (rational choice) theory,[1] which has greatly influenced

---

[1] This theory dominated the academia and political science studies for sometime and has left the important legacy of understanding political behaviour through economic perspective. See Cohn (1999).

thinking about public administration in market economies (Hay 2004; Ostrom and Ostrom 1971).

The perspective of public choice theory painted a dismal picture of governmental action. On the one hand, politicians were so fixated on winning elections that short-term policies were followed, which lacked ideological or visionary content. Bureaucrats, on whom the politicians relied on for implementing policies, were themselves preoccupied to serve their own self-interest of preserving their perks and privileges. So the whole system was myopic—largely because of the fixation of politicians on elections. It was biased towards constant expansion, mostly because of pressure from organized interests and pandering by elected leaders. And it was ossified, primarily because of resistance from powerful bureaucrats and the political influence of their clients (Roberts 2010: 11). The public choice proponents produced an analysis of government not by considering the nature of goods produced but the way the government produces them (Dardot and Laval 2013: 235). They further argued that state action must be submitted to economic analysis not only to discriminate between agenda and non-agenda, but also between ways of accomplishing the agenda (Dardot and Laval 2013: 216). Reducing costs while in delivering public goods and services became the operating criterion for evaluating state operations.

Within the prevailing setting of failures of state-led development and rise of liberalism, the theory of public choice reinforced the idea of moving away from bureaucracy as the prime instrument of implementing public policy. This perspective, emerging in the late 1960s and early 1970s, argued, on the basis of its analysis, 'that under the current administrative system public agencies are institutionally incapable of representing the demands of individual citizens' (Chandler and Plano 1988: 105), and 'since the citizen is a *consumer* of government goods and services, administrative responsiveness to individual citizen demands would be increased by creating a market system for governmental activities based on micro-economic theory'. The argument of public choice theorists to move away from the traditional system of public administration drew strength from the assumptions of myopia of politicians, resistance of bureaucracy to serve public interest and, thus, inability to serve the citizen. The crucial decision-maker was the individual, who, as a rational person, served his self-interests. As Cohn (1999) has shown, the influence of the location of the individual in social, cultural, or historical contexts on decisions was completely ignored.

In 1992, Osborne and Gaebler, drawing from the experience of the American government and with ideological footing in public choice theory, forcefully articulated the idea of 'reinventing government'—an idea that made a huge impact on policymakers and scholars across the world. This was the time when the governments, facing financial crunch, were struggling to find resources to implement welfare programmes and became very receptive to the idea of parting with some functions of the state and giving them over to the private sector and lessen their own burden. The two authors distinguished between steering and rowing—between policy decisions and service delivery—and argued that 'governments that focus on steering actively shape their communities, states and nations. They make more policy decisions. They put more social and economic institutions into motion' (Osborne and Gaebler 1992: 32). In contrast, governments preoccupied with service delivery often abdicate this steering function. Rowing function can be outsourced, contracted out, while the governments direct their attention to steering function, which has to be performed in partnership with other actors in society. They strongly advocated that the governments shed their role of monopolizing the functions of steering and rowing and seek partnership with the other actors in society to perform them. This had a strong impact on the practice of public administration and an approach labeled as 'new public management' (NPM) emerged.[2]

The fundamental logic in this exposition of reinventing government is that there is no difference between management in the public sector and private sector. Public sector pays too much attention to the political leader while ignoring the importance of the role of manager, who, as head of organization, must be seen like a chief executive officer (CEO). If the manager could be released from the control of the political leader and the constraints that politics places on management, then the system will perform better (Peters 2003).

This formulation has many implications, particularly in terms of autonomy and accountability. Like CEOs in the private sector, clear goals need to be established for them to accomplish and they should be accountable for achieving them. This shifts the focus of accountability to performance indicators and thus away from political institutions leading to demand for autonomy of the organization to perform. Efficiency is seen in economic terms and therefore private managerial practices need to be adopted in running public organizations.

Public administration began to be seen as public management, which was based on a strong anti-state, pro-privatization plank. Manning (2001) thinks that new public management is a 'slippery term' providing a menu of choices rather than a single option and emphasizes that 'dishes on offer are largely quasi-contractual and attitudinal'. Lane (2000: 307) suggests that NPM is based on two assumptions that have led to contractualism to become the operational policy. These assumptions are that of separating demand from supply—meaning if demand exists then it can be met by any source of supply; and second, for greater efficiency, greater competition

---

[2] Peters (2003: 11) thinks that no specific date can be assigned when the ideas of NPM emerged, but one might date the beginning of the tide with rise of Reagan, Thatcher, and Mulroney.

must be promoted among the suppliers. Consequently, contracting out government services enhances efficiency, and government should give greater attention to writing contracts, formalizing terms of tenders, or auctions. This again can be best handled by managers (CEOs) who have expertise, autonomy to act, and are free from political control.

Another set of reforms that illustrates many of the postulates of NPM is the creation of semi-autonomous agencies in service delivery. A new breed of agencies called executive agencies emerged that had a semi-autonomous status, having greater flexibility in taking decisions than those lying in the departmental hierarchy. Policymakers see major advantage in them for being independent of day-to-day political control and thus pursuing the cause of efficiency with professionalism and expertise. The emphasis is on getting things done. As far as accountability is concerned, these agencies are seen as autonomous of ministerial control but held responsible for achieving their goals and objectives. Such agencies did exist earlier as non-departmental bodies, but they have now acquired a slogan value such as 'privatization' 'corporatization' (Wettenhall 2006: 619).

Among the countries that went in boldly to reform the government through contractualization was New Zealand. It went to extraordinary lengths to create conditions under which formal contracts were negotiated and enforced. It restructured many departments to decouple policy functions from the delivery of services. Contract-like arrangements were extended to policy advice as well, so that ministers could opt to obtain information and ideas from consultancies and other external agencies (see Schick 1998).

NPM had a strong influence on the thinking of governments attempting administrative reforms all over the world. But the need to be cautious in adopting its menu was expressed again and again. Schick (1998) from the World Bank wrote to say that New Zealand's reforms were preceded by the existence of successful management practices and several other advances in the market sector. He has argued that greater the shortcomings in the country's established management practices, the less suitable the reforms (1998: 124). Manning (2001) of the World Bank also mentions the dubious record of the success of NPM strategies and argues that where governments are motivated and there is high level of public expectations, reforms succeed. He suggests that one lesson from NPM 'adventure' is fundamental: there are no silver bullets. He thinks the legacy of new public management may lie more in initiating fresh thinking.

More important were critical evaluations of market-based reforms for public administration. Critics were not only disputing comparison of managerial practices in for-profit organizations but also promoting them as if they had universal application. What was ignored was the 'public' part of public administration. As Pierre (2009b) suggests, there are two kinds of perceptions of public bureaucracy. One is that it is all about service production. In this perspective, public bureaucracy is seen as crippled by hierarchy, political control, input-based resource allocation, and lack of expertise in efficient design of organizations and their management. In this perspective, these public organizations stand to lose in comparison to private organizations. The other image of public administration is that it is first and foremost a structure created to ensure legality, equality, and legal security in the implementation of public policy and, more broadly, to serve as a keystone of democratic governance. Even though these may be stylized perceptions, Pierre emphasizes that legality and equal treatment remain the core values of public administration. As Peters puts it, 'As government loses control over functions considered to be public, it may lose the ability to effectively direct the society, it may lose the steering ability that constitutes the root of what we call government' (quoted in Pierre 2009a).

The defining themes of market-based reforms of public administration have been bringing the issues of efficiency and economy in to public discourse. The contestation is about the impact on nature of state and its role in society. It needs to be recognized that although citizens demand efficient and economical public services, they demand them in a transparent, equitable, and accountable fashion. They have a right to hold their governments responsible and have their rights protected. Thus, as Minogue et al. (1998: 5) point out, issues of accountability, control, responsiveness, transparency, and participation are as important as issues of economy and efficiency. Governance reforms attempted to respond to these concerns.

GOVERNANCE: BEYOND NPM

The vocabulary of reform in public administration began to change. The idea of market-based reforms and issues of economy and efficiency began to be encapsulated in the theme of good governance that became prominent in public discourse from 1990s. It drew attention to a whole range of issues concerning processes of policymaking and authoritative structures. It was more than sound management of public affairs for it placed lot of emphasis on performance, whoever the actors be in delivering public goods and services. The World Bank and the IMF, followed by other donor agencies, took the lead in conceptualizing good governance and using it to intervene in the governance of recipient countries. Today it is a buzzword used freely in most publications emanating from donor agencies and academics and plan and policy documents in India. It is heavily relied upon to explain developmental outcomes. International and multilateral aid-giving agencies have adopted it as a general guiding principle to improve the capability of the recipient countries to handle development assistance better and utilize it more efficiently.

What the concept of governance did was to redefine public sphere in neoliberal terms and blurred the public–private boundaries for the implementation of public policies. However, there is very little agreement on its core idea and less and less on how it could be applied more concretely. In any case, improving a country's capability to utilize aid better or work for improved developmental performance does not connote the same meanings to everyone. The meanings range from following liberal economic policies, to strengthening and reforming market institutions, to building capacities of public institutions to perform, to encouraging democratic participation through strengthening civil society institutions and so on. Some meanings are concerned with reducing the role of the state in economic activities, others with strengthening state institutions to promote the role of market, and yet others relate to the encouragement of democracy and participation.[3] It is for this reason that Chakrabarty and Bhattacharya (2008: 4) argue that 'governance is a conceptual muddle'.

In this web of many meanings of governance, there is a baseline agreement that governance refers to the development of governing styles in which boundaries between and within public and private sectors have become blurred (Stoker 1998:155). What were previously indisputably roles of government are now increasingly seen as more common, generic, societal problems which can not only be resolved by political institutions, but also by other actors. The main point is that political institutions no longer exercise a monopoly over the orchestration of governance (Pierre 2000: 4). The concept of governance indicates a shift away from well-established notions of the way government sought to resolve social issues through a top-down approach.

---

[3] Scott (1998: 60) suggests that the complex language of governance is perhaps the most effective guarantee that a social world, easily accessible to an insider, will remain opaque to an outsider. In effect, those who cannot grasp the language are rendered mute and marginal. Offe (2009: 554) also contends that the success of its dissemination contrasts with the informational value of the term; when one refers to something as an instance of 'governance', one has not expressed much—possibly because of the multiple meanings.

The idea of non-state actors working with state to make policy and deliver services in partnership became very influential. Notion of governance strengthened the idea of network relationships of three actors—state, market, and civil society—and it became its core thrust in changing the practice of public administration. Governance in its *avatar* during the neoliberal era is seen as an interactive process where government may like to impose its will but its acceptance will depend on compliance and action of others. One institution depends on another, and this is what Stoker refers to as 'power dependence'. In this relationships and networks of state and non-state institutions, no one single institution can dominate. The nature of relationships and networks will depend on processes of exchange in particular cases. The monopoly of political institutions in providing services is diluted; the private sector and institutions of civil society fill in the space previously occupied by these institutions. New forms of institutions emerge and this finds expression in the blurring of boundaries between the public and the private sectors. A range of participative agencies arise that respond to collective concerns.

Sorenson and Torfing (2004: 5), in reviewing the literature on governance networks, suggest that governance readily adopts the network metaphor in order to account for the multidimensional patterns of interaction between political actors, but it shifts the focus from the question of representation of vertical interests to the question of the role of horizontal networks in processes of societal governance. The vantage point is not the interested organization and its attempt to gain influence in public policy through formal and informal contacts with the central decision makers. Rather, the focus is on the production of public policy and the contribution of public and private actors to it. As Rhodes (2006: 426) points out, 'Policy networks are sets of formal institutional and informal linkages between governmental and other actors structured around shared if endlessly negotiated beliefs and interests in public policymaking and implementation. These actors are interdependent and policy emerges from the interactions between them.' Policy networks are also strategic alliances forged around common agendas of mutual advantage through collective action (Hay and Richards 2000).

At the formal level, policy networks have emerged as public institutions where interactions between government, business, and civil society can take place. These interactions lead to policy outputs. In operational terms, governments have instituted advisory bodies and various kinds of councils where representatives of government and the other two actors—business and civil society—are members. Such policy networks are different from lobby groups whose role was to influence government to get outputs in their favour.

At the informal level, governance means opening up of government activities to non-government actors. It is no longer a preserve of hierarchical decision-making, which is often secretive and closed. The three actors—state, market, and civil society—interact more frequently in the public domain and attempt to formulate public policies together. This is distinct from an understanding of lobby groups who tend to influence the government to frame/bend policy in their favour. It is a fundamental change towards a more open government that is willing to listen and become one participant in among the three in policymaking.

Apart from policy networks, there can be operational networks too. These networks are implementation tools delivering public goods and services that one single actor cannot deliver. Increasingly, the government has adopted the mode of seeking cooperation of one or the other actor in implementing programmes of public interest. Such cooperation has taken the form of what has come to be popularly known as public–private partnership. This type of partnership is widely being promoted as a strategy of governance in delivering goods and services in many sectors.

Governance agenda then underlines the curbing of the role of state and expanding the space for market and competition.

Competition is accepted as a powerful tool and an essential dimension of economic, political, and social life. In extolling the virtues of the market and competition and in laying stress on the past failures of state, governance agenda virtually condemns the state of having suppressed the energies of a society. Because the state is an alien oppressor, the curtailment of state activities becomes a people friendly, democratic venture, almost to the extent that state contraction or dissatisfaction is presented as synonymous with democratization. Its emphasis on civil society and its institutions have to be seen in the context of strengthening democracy and in constructing an informal sector that can harness people's entrepreneurship through community institutions and inter-personal relationships. In the good governance discourse, democracy emerges as the necessary political framework for successful economic development, and within this discourse democracy and economic liberalism are conceptually linked: bad governance equals state intervention; good governance equals democracy and economic liberalism.

Thus, governance reform does not merely mean establishing new implementation institutions that are modelled on the managerial practices of the private sector. It also means adoption of practices of participation and democratic accountability. It is on this foundation that governance reforms are promoted and the World Bank identifies associated characteristics to evaluate whether governance is good or bad.

It is also for this reason that in the agenda of good governance, the conceptualization of civil society proceeds on the assumption that power and exploitation is associated with the state, while freedom and liberty falls in the realm of civil society. This leads to a kind of romantic view of civil society where the existence of institutions outside the state becomes a sufficient basis to assume that state power is curbed and greater democratization is taking place. It is in this perspective that the concept of civil society carries with it a notion of something worthy and of value. It is considered good in itself and its creation a worthy goal to be pursued. Those promoting the ideology of liberalization helped the international donors and governments of the Third World shape an uncritical view of the civil society and persuaded them to believe that it can be created though their aid and policies of support. The view that 'civil society could do no wrong and there was nothing it could not do' was widely accepted among donor agencies. Non-governmental Organizations (NGOs) sprang up like mushrooms offering to strengthen civil society and as civil organizations in their own right. In many cases they claimed to speak on behalf of civil society at large. In the field of development, the role of NGOs was strengthened through donor aid and policies.

Governance as a concept thus began to encompass a wide array of issues relating to the restructuring of state–market–society relationships. What all this has meant is that governance reforms agenda is very wide and complex. It ranges from reforming the entire gamut of state machinery for improving delivery of goods and services, strengthening civil society, to becoming an effective partner in socio-economic endeavours and strengthening market mechanisms for greater efficiency. Existing institutions needed to be improved and new institutions created where none existed. This is a daunting challenge, a challenge that India is facing with uneven success.

What is significant to our discussion is that the notion of good governance carried on the agenda of neoliberal reforms and widened the scope of new public management. An ideological pillar of all these reforms was that the provision of public services is better when the provision is made by the private sector. Moreover, with the adjective 'good' added to it, it became unmistakably clear that the concept of 'good governance' could be used to invite judgement about how the country, city, or agency concerned was being governed; it enabled the raising of evaluative questions about proper procedures, transparency, the quality and processes of decision-making, and other such matters (Doornbos 2001: 94).

Within the neoliberal perspective, administrative reforms began to be tied up with shrinking of state and increasing role of private sector in implementing public policies. Adoption of private sector managerial practices with emphasis on economy and efficiency became the goals to be pursued by public agencies. Institutional transformation took place to accommodate these goals. While earlier efforts at administrative reforms world over were attempts to make the Weberian–Wilsonian framework of hierarchy and neutrality more flexible and responsive to social needs, governance reforms offered an alternative model. Governance reforms, on the one hand, assumed that public administration can be improved by focusing on results. Private-sector management vocabulary of performance budgeting, results-oriented management, and outcomes measurement came into vogue (Miller and Fox 2007:13). On the other hand, shedding state functions and partnering with business and civil society to achieve state goals became symbolic of expanding and deepening democracy.[4] Whatever be the merits of the two ideas, most countries' recipients of international aid, particularly from the World Bank and the IMF, found them attractive and were open to adopt them.

The recounting of these ideas originating in Western thinking and experience is important because it appears that without going through a formal reform process, governments in India are incorporating them to bring substantive changes in the way public services get delivered in the country. From the time that Paul Appleby was invited for suggesting reforms, it has been a journey through a Western maze of ideas and practices that are being applied to bring about administrative changes in developing countries. Policy prescriptions emerged from the experience of developed countries.

---

[4] The World Bank, in promoting ideas about good governance, calls for accountability, transparency, and rule of law for sustainable development. See World Bank (1994).

Evaluation of these experiments did not impact the reform policies. Ironically, most of the time, such evaluations were not even undertaken. Once again, the agenda of governance reforms inspired by the World Bank and other donor agencies is being pursued, but the learning from the past is being given a go-by. The World Bank has played primary role through its 'soft power' in influencing the thinking about good governance world over. Papers have been published and seminars and discussions organized to focus on this idea. In an influential contribution, it has been instrumental in creating benchmarks in good governance to rank countries (Dearra and Plane 2014).

In the phase before the neoliberal economic reforms were introduced, the reform movement was generated largely by the Ford Foundation and UNDP. These agencies provided funding for training, exposing policymakers to new ideas, and provided initial resources to help establish new institutions of training and education. During the post-neoliberal reform period, multilateral funding agencies—The World Bank, the IMF, and the Asian Development Bank, for example—have taken over this role. These agencies deploy conditions of implementation for programme funding. Acceptance of reform agenda becomes part of the larger policy framework of globalization. This is a major change in the strategy of promoting reforms. What is significant is that this strategy leaves the traditional administrative system alone and seeks to impose a new set of institutions parallel to it.

But this strategy presents major challenges: in all sectors of delivery of public goods and services, there are now parallel institutions—the government, private institutions, and institutions of public–private partnership. Delivery of public goods is no more the exclusive domain of state. The impact of this strategy in recasting public administration in India by imposing an administrative reform agenda from the top and without making the traditional administrative system congenial to it is yet to fully unfold itself.

There are three important pillars of neoliberal governance reforms: One includes shedding functions and reducing the scope of the state. This leads to privatization of services. Second is creating policy networks of government and the private sector to build cooperation in policymaking. Third is changing the implementation process by creating institutions of public–private partnership to implement programmes. We turn our attention to them and their experience in India now.

6   Shedding Functions as Reform

It is common knowledge that economic reforms introduced in the early 1990s in India dismantled the planning system of the earlier three decades and set in motion neoliberal policies for development.[1] Many of these policies were derived from the conditions laid down in loan arrangements from the World Bank and the IMF. These loans had become imperative to tide over the debt crisis that had prompted the government to take loans to pay off debts in the first place and thus restore financial credibility to India during 1991–3. An important lesson that was being taught in structural adjustment loans and financial stabilization of IMF programmes was to cut down on financial deficits and keep them under some stipulated proportion of the budget. As a matter of fact, the performance of the government began to be measured on the basis of fiscal deficit that it budgeted in a financial year. Reduction of fiscal deficit involved two aspects—reducing expenditures and raising revenues. Raising revenues was a more challenging option and, therefore, the government in India took recourse to reducing expenditures. The neoliberal reforms together with this strategy also envisaged reducing subsidies and downsizing the government.

---

[1] In 2014, the Planning Commission itself was abolished, yielding place to National Institute for Transforming India-NITI AYOG.

The tenets of NPM were already laying foundations of governmental reforms through downsizing and narrowing the scope of state activities The call for reducing fiscal deficit seemed the right opportunity to raise the populist slogan of 'less government more governance'. The first step in this direction came from the policy of downsizing the government, which translated into both reducing the number of government employees as well as narrowing the scope of state activities or 'shrinking the state'.

The Fifth Pay Commission was the first pay commission set up after liberalization in 1991 to recommend reduction in staff strength of the central government. In the three years following the submission of this report, the staff strength did not change remarkably, but the effort was to keep the number stable. In 1997, it was 38.97 lakhs (1 lakh equals 100,000) and came down to 37.01 lakhs in 2006. The Seventh Pay Commission suggested in its report presented in 2016 that the rate of growth of employee strength has not been abnormally high, though the actual number has registered an increase to 38.19 lakhs in 2014.

The Seventh Pay Commission has, however, attempted to correct the perception that the government was fat and flabby. The central government had 139 employees per 1 lakh population as compared to 668 in the United States. Possibly the image of a bloated government stems from the easy visibility of C and D category of employees.

CONTRACTING OUT SERVICES

Contracting out services has been an important mode of downsizing government and has taken place at various levels. The Fifth Pay Commission suggested that a large number of services, which are currently being performed in-house, can be conveniently outsourced to the private sector. Keeping up with this recommendation, many services of housekeeping, maintenance services, transport, and so on have been contracted out or outsourced. In government parlance, the levels of staff most affected by this are usually clubbed together in the C and D categories. This category of staff forms a very large part of the government workforce and is usually semi-skilled and semi-literate. Contracting out services is a form of privatization that has become a politically popular strategy in the neoliberal framework of governance reforms. When third parties deliver more public services, the government needs less workers. Contracting out services also exposes public services to competition, which is the cornerstone of efficiency proponents. However, Van Dyke (2003) warns us of the many challenges that this mode of reforms faces and argues that it is more of a political than an economic act. Its success not only depends on the extent of competition that takes place, but also on the government's managerial capacity to oversee its performance and enforce accountability.

In the Indian context, contracting out services has had another significant implication. Anecdotal evidence suggests that the emerging system of competitive provision of services has been detrimental to the interests of the contract labour, which has been deprived of the facilities that government employees receive in terms of social security benefits. Work hours are longer in contract jobs and exploitative wages are fixed. Persons in contract jobs are also not assured of a long tenure, and those working at the lower levels of the governmental system are particularly vulnerable. It is probably due to these reasons that a regular job in the government is preferred and there is always a demand to fill vacancies at the C and D levels of government hierarchy.[2]

[2] The government appears to be conscious of this situation and claims in a wider context that the interests of contract labourers in terms of wages and other service conditions are safeguarded under the Contract Labour (Abolition and Regulation) Act of 1970 and the rules frames within it. However, the government is also conscious of the fact that provisions of many laws enacted for safeguarding the interests of contract labour are not observed in actual practice. The Ministry of Finance issued a letter in 2013

If the effort was to reduce employment at the C and D levels of government, the policy had a contrary effect on the employment of personnel at higher levels. Indeed, the positions at the higher levels of hierarchy have multiplied. During the period 1997–2000, the number of persons at the higher positions in the hierarchy, from secretaries to government to deputy secretaries, increased from 1371 to 1691, an increase of around 20 per cent. The authorized strength of the IAS has witnessed a steady rise. It had 5,159 personnel in 2001 that rose to 5,261 in 2005, 5,671 in 2009, and 6,270 in 2012. Thus, from the time the call for downsizing the government was made by the Fifth Pay Commission, there has been a steady rise in the authorized strength of the IAS. Again, this has been happening when experts and professionals are being employed in greater numbers by ministries and departments of government.

A recent report mentions that a large number of consultants are working with the Health ministry and the possible figure is that of 363. Most of these consultants/experts are sponsored by external agencies who are funding the plethora of new schemes being implemented by the ministry. Such has been the practice for many years, since the acquisition of schemes has grown while government has not sanctioned any new positions to implement them (*Times of India* 24 June 2015). In a move that is the first of its kind, the Ministry of External Affairs has also announced its intention to allow for lateral entry of experts at senior-level diplomatic positions. This again is seen as a method to compensate for the shortfall in positions in diplomatic service. The practice of employing non-state experts and professionals in economic ministries and the Planning Commission has been in vogue for a long time. In 2006,

---

asking all ministries and departments to take action where there is non-compliance of these provisions. See the circular available at www.cbec. govt.in/deptt_offcr/circ-dept/labourlaw-compliance.pdf.

the Ministry of Finance issued guidelines for the appointment of consultants in ministries under the Government of India. In terms of service conditions, these guidelines made a distinction between those who would be under the payroll of the government and those who would be paid by the external funding agencies and came in as part of the aid package. Thus, the system has now been formalized.

It is important to see the entry of professionals and experts as consultants and strictly outside the civil service system as a reflection of two things. One is the inability to professionalize the civil service itself. The civil service remains a generalist civil service where careers are made on the number of diverse jobs that one holds. Second, it is also a reflection of the spirit of 'reinventing government'. With health or education services being increasingly contracted out, the government has taken upon steering function more seriously.

The paradox is that in spite of contracting out services and employment of outsiders, the number of employees at both lower and higher levels has not shown a significant decline. There is contracting out at junior levels and contracting in at higher ones. The employment of consultants and experts at higher implementation planning and policy levels also raises issues of accountability and conflict of interest. Many of the senior-level consultants have either served or are on deputation from external agencies whose avowed goal is to influence government policy in the sectors in which they serve.[3]

This method of downsizing has really thwarted the spirit of the reform of reducing the government flab. At the higher level, there

[3] It was reported that foreign-funded consultants working with Union government for more than three years had been asked to quit by December 2016. This decision is seen as an effort to reduce the influence of the international agencies and the NGOs on public policy and not necessarily an effort to professionalize the existing civil service. The government also feels that much confidential information is also leaked out by the foreign consultants (*Hindustan Times* 6 April 2016).

is not only an increase in senior-level positions but also greater employment of persons on contract. Employees on contract, some funded by external agencies, are not on the payroll of the government and thus do not add formally to the numbers of central government employees. The size of the government is thus not reflected in the number of employees.

SEMI-AUTONOMOUS AGENCIES

Another form of outsourcing of services has been by farming out government functions to semi-autonomous agencies. It is not as if this strategy was not used earlier but it has intensified in recent years as governance reforms have taken shape. Widely popular in Britain, Australia, and New Zealand, these agencies have become institutions of functional decentralization in contrast to territorial decentralization. A large part of the British civil service soon found itself relocated in these agencies—a development which attracted much attention around the world and had considerable model value as many other countries embarked on a new programme of creating agencies with some degree of resemblance to the British prototype (Wettenhall 2005: 616). The motivation of creating such institutions lies squarely in the ideas of NPM in which efficiency and economy reign supreme. The assumption is that such agencies will have the autonomy of employing best managerial practices without the encumbrances of interference in day-to-day politics and bureaucratic procedures.

In India, such institutions are multiplying, particularly in cases where the source of funding is external donor agencies. The concerns of economy and efficiency are combined with the recognition that the government has failed to provide these services in its own set-up. Donor agencies also find it easier to hold these agencies accountable for the funds disbursed to them. Many new centrally sponsored programmes and new local government initiatives have been lodged in this mode. The government is quick to show its urgency in carrying out specific tasks by establishing such agencies as Special Purpose Vehicles and calling it the mission mode of implementation.

These institutions are registered as societies under the Societies Registration Act, 1860, and function on the basis of by-laws framed by its members. A very large number of initiatives at the local level have been undertaken in this mode. These institutions are popular as they can operate their own bank accounts and remain outside the purview of government audit systems.

At the local level, several kinds of contradictions have developed while promoting such agencies outside the realm of government bureaucracy or constitutionally mandated democratic institutions. Within the new governance discourse, great faith was placed on NGOs as engines of development, and donor agencies began to direct funds and resources directly to them without governmental mediation. This led to the strengthening of NGOs and support in creating them where they did not exist at the local level. Most of these NGOs were linked to registered societies at state level and enjoyed great deal of freedom from bureaucratic and legislative control. They are not linked to panchayats (local democratic institution charged with similar functions) and not accountable to them. The use of many natural resources is managed through user committees, which are participatory but restricted to stakeholders. Separate funds are earmarked for them. What is happening then is that much of the developmental activities are taking place outside the panchayat system. Thus, as Chandrashekhar (2011) points out, while NGOs are flush with funds, panchayats do not have the wherewithal to perform even the minimum maintenance functions of the assets and utilities of the village.

The proliferation of such semi-autonomous institutions has another implication for the erosion of the significance of the traditional administrative system. These agencies have set targets, flexible working procedures, and adequate financing, and have the flexibility to choose efficient administrators to man them. These characteristics, as Sharma (2013) points out, hardly get internalized in the regular administrative system. On the contrary, these agencies serve to attract more skilled bureaucrats from the regular administrative system. If these agencies were limited to implement some specific headline projects, they could act as exemplars, but making them basic tools of governance pushes out the concerns of intrinsic administrative reform.

The other, possibly more significant, problem, as Singh (2016: 23) outlines, is that these societies are outside the governance structure of the state and hence not bound by the principles of the Constitution and the values and ideals enshrined in it. Instead, he emphasizes, they rely on by-laws that are often self-written contracts that govern these societies. On the basis of his field studies, he has shown that it may not be uncommon to find many of such user committees debarring other villagers' access to wood or forest products in forest committees.

Many of the NGOs implementing social projects have taken the shape of user committees with the aim of providing participation to the beneficiaries of a particular service. Thus, these committees are found in areas of minor irrigation, education, forest management, water supply, and so on. International agencies view user committees as a mechanism to give local people greater say over the development decisions that affect them. In the context of dispersal of power and reliance on civil society, inclusion of organizations as stakeholders in a particular activity is viewed as decentralization.

The government is increasingly resorting to this institutional framework for shedding its responsibility of water supply in both rural as well as urban areas. The responsibility is being handed over to community organizations and private companies. This is a phenomenon that is not confined to India alone but is happening all over the world as the sweep of neoliberal reforms widens itself. During the 1990s, some of the world's largest multinationals

(Bechtel, Enron, Vivandi) began expanding operations and ownership of water systems on a global scale; the largest water company
now has over 100 million customers worldwide (Bakker 2011: 2).

Water privatization is a significant part of the neoliberalization
agenda being promoted by private donors, aid-giving agencies, and
international financial institutions. The World Commission on Water
formed in 1998 with the support of the World Bank and the United
Nations and consisting of eminent policymakers belonging to the
field of politics, government, and business set the ball rolling when
it recommended that due to heavy investments required to supply
water to the poor on a regular basis, the services should be privatized,
subsidies be cut, and water costs be recovered from the consumers
(see Goldman 2007 for the evolution of privatization policy and the
role of the World Bank). Its report warned that 'without full cost
pricing the present vicious cycle of waste, inefficiency and lack of
service for the poor will continue'. Private parties also 'will not invest
unless they can be assured of a reasonable return on their investments'
(quoted in Goldman 2007: 791). Push towards privatization became
a business enterprise and The World Business Council for Sustainable
Development had this to say:

> Providing water services to the poor presents a business opportunity.
> New pipes, pumps, measurement and monitoring devices, and bill-
> ing and record keeping systems will be required to modernize and
> expand water infrastructure. Industry not directly related to the pro-
> vision of water services will be able to enter new markets because
> water for production, and to sustain a productive workforce, will
> be available. Thus this program has the possibility of creating huge
> employment and sales opportunities for large and small businesses
> alike. (quoted in Goldman 2007: 793)

What is happening is that a powerful lobby for reforms in the
water sector has emerged, which is being facilitated by the World
Bank through its loans and aid conditionalities. The endeavours of
this lobby are being fuelled by the failure of governments to provide

clean and potable water to all its citizens on a regular basis. Water crisis in the developing countries is being treated as a technical issue to which the efficiency of the private sector is the answer. It is not being recognized that water crisis is inextricably tied up with the political groupings and their influence on policymaking. For the urban elite water is usually available and is relatively cheap; it is the urban poor who suffer from daily hardship due to scarcity of water. In this pursuit of relying on the private sector, the policymakers also seem to neglect the fact that efficiency can be achieved by ignoring social policy goals and not only through flexible financial and engineering practices (Bakker 2011: 73).

Privatization of water supply came a little late on India's policy agenda, and it was only in 2002 that a National Water Policy was first adopted, which recognized the role of the private sector in water supply. It mentioned:

> Private sector participation should be encouraged in planning, development and management of water resources projects for diverse uses, wherever feasible. Private sector may help in introducing innovative ideas, generating financial resources and introducing corporate management and improving service efficiency and accountability to users. Depending on situations, various combinations of private sector participation, in building, owning, operating, leasing and transferring of water resources facilities may be considered. (Government of India 2002: para 13)

A study by Manthan Adhyayan Kendra, Madhya Pradesh (Dwivedi et al. 2007), has extensively documented the Indian policy initiatives since the exhortation towards privatization in the declaration of 2002. Pointing out that the early initiatives were in the area of industrial water supply, the study shows that water supply projects now cover a number of cities throughout the country. According to the Manthan report, privatization projects have been installed or are in pipeline in 29 cities of the country. As in the world over, protests over privatization have also been rising, delaying, or stalling projects.

The scenario is that agencies such as Asian Development Bank and the World Bank are pushing for reforms on possibly reluctant states through their loans and aid. In turn, the Government of India and the Planning Commission are using schemes such as Jawaharlal Nehru National Urban Renewal Mission (JNNURM) to encourage states to adopt the policies. The risk of protests is laid at the door of state governments to handle. As one has put graphically: People rise up angry every morning.

In a scheme of rural water supply, it has been argued that the Swajal water project in Uttar Pradesh has demonstrated that community driven development for rural infrastructure could be cost effective and sustainable (Singh 2007:186–219). The management of the project was located outside the government and water board. The Project Management Unit (PMU) was an autonomous registered society. The PMU and the local village communities in the form of village and sanitation committees took the help of NGOs for both hardware and software support. The members of these committees were representatives of the stakeholder group (water users, NGOs giving technical support, and the government) that bypassed the gram panchayat. Singh (2007: 194) has argued that the Swajal water project demonstrated for the first time that not only could state funds be efficiently managed by village committees, but that it was also possible to recover the entire operation and maintenance cost for rural supply projects from village user committees.

Delhi began its efforts to privatize water supply a couple of years ago as more and more cities adopted these policies throughout the country. Incentives to do so came from the central government. *The Hindustan Times* (10 August 2012) reported that the Twelfth Five-Year Plan (2012–17) had increased the allocation for Delhi state by around 50 per cent. But this increase came at a price. It demanded privatization of capital's water distribution and pushed Delhi towards it. The response of the chief minister to the panel was: 'We will ensure 24 by 7 water supply with public–private partnership.'

Delhi Jal Board was constituted under the Delhi Water Board Act 1998 and is responsible for planning, designing, and execution of water supply and wastewater management in the National Capital Region. The projects that the board has prepared and are in operation are based on the assumption that the improved managerial measures and reliance on privatization in some form or the other is the solution. It is also based on the fact that tariffs must rise, gradually leading to 'full cost recovery'. International agencies such as the World Bank and Asian Development Bank have had a strong influence on the Delhi Jal Board in charting out operational details of the projects. These agencies have also influenced the appointment of consultants through loan and funding conditions. The Japan International Cooperation Agency (JICA) is another agency that provides financial assistance for some of the projects.[4]

In 2012, the Nagpur municipality handed over its water supply to a subsidiary of the French water corporation Veolia for 25 years. As the government pushes for more private sector investments—urban infrastructure and development of smart cities—the Nagpur model is being showcased for emulation. However, it appears that the ground reality is different. Lacking any formal evaluation of the contract and its implementation, there have been allegations of corruption, increases in water tariffs four times, cost overruns, and delays in plugging leaks.

Privatization of water supply has considerable international backing insisting on privatization and recovering costs of supply so that efficiency in operations can be gained. This formulation has been contested and Delhi saw a number of public protests for failure to supply water as projected and neglecting the weaker sections of society whose ability to pay was limited. Water services were handed over to a private operator in Latur a few years ago,

---

[4] See more details on privatization of Delhi water supply in Mathur (2012).

but the municipality had to take it back when protests showed that there were increases in water tariffs without any improvement in water services. No effort has been made to assess the cost efficiency of contracting out services or its efficiency in reaching out to all sections of consumers. Taking away the responsibility of supplying water from the government made water a commercial commodity to be paid for and thus excluding those who could not do so. Water was no more a right of the citizen.

Another illustration of the way services are being contracted out has been given by Nayanika Mathur (Mathur and Bear 2015: 22–4) from her field study in a district in Uttarakhand. Implementing NREGA, a colossal rural employment programme, required high levels of bureaucratic action. The expansion of traditional bureaucracy would inflate the cost of the welfare programme and also push it into a quagmire of old practices. What the government did was to superimpose a set of professionals, from diverse fields, who provided all the support services such as computer work and so on and the engineers among them designed infrastructure projects. These professionals were contracted out by a government-controlled NGO and thus were not part of the traditional hierarchy.

The creation of a parallel organization led to fragmentation of work, leading to conflicts between the 'outsiders' and the 'insiders'. These conflicts have had a detrimental impact on the implementation of the programme. The point to stress is that the desire of the government is to provide a more cost effective and efficient system without revamping the traditional system of administration and its ethos. This is leading to unintended consequences.

In another twist in the terminology, many of the schemes funded by central government are being implemented in what has come to be known as 'mission mode' through registered societies. These societies are registered at the national level and then spread out with agencies at the local levels. Implementation committees are formed at the district and lower levels. Based on the experience of

Karnataka, Chandrashekhar (2011) points out that the society mode of implementation has also created a parallel bureaucracy for implementing Sarva Shiksha Abhiyan, which has its own set of problems resulting in considerable confusion regarding performance of the tasks of educational bureaucracy. Sarva Shiksha Abhiyan is being implemented in mission mode through registered state level societies which effectively bypass the decision-making process entrusted to elected representatives.

The mission mode as exemplified in the Sarva Shiksha Abhiyan is an attempt to place educational reforms and goal of achieving universal elementary education on to a fast track. It appears that this education reform activity is undertaken not by reforming the educational administrative system, but by setting up a parallel system that bypasses political institutions and processes, redeploys bureaucracy, and provides for independent fund flows. Decisions are taken by the District Implementation Committees that take care of developmental functions leaving routine matters to traditional educational administration, which continues to be afflicted by paucity of development funds and works in the traditional mode.

The path of establishing societies and user committees to achieve developmental goals seems to be followed in every sector. Many of these sectors are under the domain of panchayats and their responsibilities are getting eroded. Participation is taking a different meaning by focusing attention on single tasks and concentrating on specific users of the service. Democratically elected panchayats are being bypassed in the process. Similarly, a large number of tasks are being outsourced to private agencies in the urban sector. The JNURM schemes are bypassing the duly elected urban local bodies and are being implemented through such agencies.

A major consequence of creating semi-autonomous bodies for implementing specific programmes is fragmentation of public administration in the country. The issues worst affected are those of accountability and transparency. The proponents of NPM argue that a new system of accountability is created where the agencies become accountable to the people they serve. Thus, user committees or registered society mode are answerable to their clients or customers (Pierre 2009b). Farming out public services to such agencies raises some fundamental questions about the notion of public administration where 'public' denoted not only democratic governance, but also responsiveness to citizens at large. But as Hirst (1995) reminds us, extensive use of semi-autonomous agencies owes much to the distrust of day-to-day politics and belief in the weakness of the administrative system and faith in the private sector practices and personnel to invigorate public service delivery.

RISE OF INDEPENDENT REGULATING AGENCIES

The other development in the landscape of public administration in India is the emergence of independent regulatory agencies to oversee the performance of these new institutions in the pursuit of public interest. As privatization of public services goes unabated, the concern about its ability to serve public interests also rises. Regulatory agencies are multiplying and being demanded where they do not exist to oversee that these private institutions serve public interest.

Regulation is what all governments do. This they do through a specific set of commands where regulation involves the promulgation of a binding set of rules to be applied by a body devoted to this purpose. They can regulate also by influencing behaviour through taxes and subsidies (Baldwin et al. 2013: 3). In this latter sense, regulation has always existed and exercised through government's own departments and agencies.

What is new is the setting up of independent regulatory agencies whose genesis lies in the American experience. With the increasing role of the corporate private sector in economic activities, it has become necessary for the government to safeguard citizen interests and see that the private sector serves public interest. Increasing complexities and advancement of technologies require that issues be handled by experts and they should be insulated from political interference. In addition, as government pursues goals of higher growth through increased private investment, an assurance of level playing field and continuity in policy needs to be provided.

The Second ARC points out that traditional departmental structures are not suited to play the dual role of policymaking as well as regulating the sector concerned. Independent regulatory agencies are being set up that are autonomous of the government and are staffed by experts who have domain knowledge. Such agencies have already come in the sectors of power, telecom, financial services, insurance, and so on.

Reviewing the performance of several regulatory agencies in India, Bhattacharya and Patel (2005) contend that regulatory agencies have not decreased the uncertainty that the corporate sector faces in investing in many infrastructure segments in India. Even though some independence is assured through legislation, the pattern of appointments from a pool of serving or retired civil servants does not represent a relationship of autonomy. They also suggest that because of this kind of composition, there is also the potential of regulators entrenching themselves and enlarging their regulatory jurisdiction.

Dubash (2012) points out that these agencies have been promoted by international donor agencies and have been viewed primarily as a mechanism to insulate decision-making process from politics. He further suggests these agencies have entered India through the back door and act as one more layer of the government.

On the basis of extensive work that he and his colleagues have done in the power sector, Dubash further points out that regulating agencies have been caught between the technical demands, financial health of the sector, consumer dissatisfaction arising from rising tariffs, and the intervention of government to balance the conflicting interests. They have given into government encroaching on their terrain for they have been ill-placed to resolve these issues and have merely maintained a facade of independent decision-making.

Together with sectoral regulating agencies, which are multiplying as private sector increases its role in economic activities, an over-arching legislation was passed in 2002 to establish the Competition Commission. Among its various functions, the commission aims at preventing practices that may have an adverse effect on competition and seeing that markets function for the welfare of the consumers. It has been hailed as a move towards a more modern regulatory regime with the objective of enhancing consumer welfare by sustaining competition in the market place (see *Mint* 16 June 2014). It has enforced some market discipline in sectors ranging from real estate developers and cricket organizations.

What must be emphasized at the end of this discussion is that this new institutional architecture is embedded in a major postulate of public choice theory. We have already mentioned that its perspective on political action was not flattering. The NPM institutions that emerged out of its theoretical assumptions were designed to either control the role of politicians or transfer critical decision-making functions to a group of technocrat-guardians who can take decisions on behalf of the public. What was needed was 'de-politicization' so that virtues of farsightedness, consistency, and public spiritedness could be promoted. De-politicization is done through contracts, and legislation that can give some autonomy to institutions or proscribe policy choices entirely (Roberts 2010: 5).

The new institutional architecture then seems to follow the above-mentioned framework with the attempt to give greater decision-making space to experts and technocrats through design of institutions and legislations that establish them. The actual experience of the way they work, though, is considerably influenced by the fact that these institutions are also embedded in the traditional administrative system with a dominating role of a civil service that nibbles at this autonomy and a political leadership that does not hesitate to intervene for its constituency.

7 Public–Private Partnership (PPP)
A Conceptual Perspective

Continuing the quest for setting up new institutions that could improve delivery of public goods and services, active partnership with private sector began in right earnest in the neoliberal governance framework. The partnership was based on the assumption that an institution that has an active involvement of the private sector will deploy managerial practices that will lead to efficiency and economy in the delivery of services. PPPs are seen as a response to the perceived inability of the traditional administration to be effective agents of regulation and development. The policymakers in India also saw in partnerships opportunities to attract private funds for public projects. Thus, Indian policymakers saw partnerships as a response to state failure and also as an opportunity to utilize funds and technology that was available with the private sector. The terminology that includes the term 'partnership' also appeared to be more acceptable than 'contracting out services', which had a connotation of privatization.

The emphasis on PPPs changed the pattern of governance, as well as adaptations in management practices and in perceptions regarding the role and responsibilities of different development actors in the context of globalization and liberalization. This transformation has also been termed as a pragmatic turn in official development practice, and as Utting and Zammit (2006:2) point out, 'Approaches to development interventions, and in particular the role of the private sector, are said to be driven by "what works" and less by ideology.'

PPPs appeared even more of a pragmatic turn because of the context where the financial circumstances of both the government and private sector were changing. Governments were suffering from financial crises and fiscal deficits in the 1980s while the corporate sector was doing well with good returns and technological advancement. Across the world, partnership among the three actors—state, market, and civil society—began to be promoted as a strategy of good governance. The partnerships promise to avoid duplication of efforts and are seen to draw on their complementary resources and capabilities to design more effective problem-solving mechanisms. They promise to increase responsiveness of policies and create accountability by including other actors—market and civil society—into decision-making processes. They are also presumed to improve compliance with and implementation of political decisions. In addition, the partnerships provide opportunities to the partners to learn from each other (Streets 2004). It is widely believed that networks play a significant role in the processes promoting social and economic development. Pingle (2000) has argued that shared understandings are vital for better functioning of economic decision-making. Shared understandings help overcome bureaucratic resistance and allow the state to not fall prey to social and political interests. Industrialists increase their ability to get necessary infrastructure and collective goods for future growth.

However, this optimism is not shared by many. Critics point out that these partnerships can be a strategy of the state to evade responsibility. There has been considerable belief in the proposition that 'the hierarchical governance of the society by the state is based on substantive rationality. The political values and preferences of the government—that is supposed to incarnate the will of the people—are translated into more or less detailed laws and regulations that are implemented and enforced by publicly employed bureaucracies' (Sorenson and Torfing 2004). These bureaucracies are accountable to the representatives of people who express these preferences. Networks carry the risk of weakening traditional accountability mechanisms by shifting policy decisions to the realm of partnerships that can circumvent parliamentary control (Streets 2004).

A fear that partnerships can be used by the corporate sector to embellish their own power and resources is also expressed. Galbraith also expressed this fear when he suggested, in his influential book, *The Affluent Society*, that corporates in exercising social and economic power had made the Western societies rich in private goods but poor in public goods such as mass transport, public health, low cost housing, and good schools for ordinary people (quoted in Das 2000: 86).

There have been other concerns too. Rosenau (2000: 224) quoted in Datta (2009: 74) questions the consensus in policy literature that partnerships combine the best of both the worlds of public and private and argues that if partnerships emphasize cost reduction or profit maximization at the price of significant quality compromises, vulnerable populations may not be able to respond appropriately and aggressively. There is always the risk that the poor and the marginalized groups in the population may be excluded due to pricing policies.

Despite these concerns, optimism about the partnerships is prevailing and a complex web of institutions is emerging worldwide that has a far-reaching impact on the nature of state and functioning of democracy. The notion of governance is transforming the organization of the state and its relationships with the private sector and civil society actors. Considerable amount of scholarly attention is now being devoted to analysing and debating this transformation of state and democracy. Attention is being directed towards improving the understanding of the wider public policy system in which the institutions of the government appear to be involved in processes of negotiation, bargaining, and compromise with a host of other actors.

The transformation of state hierarchical bureaucratic processes into a world of policy and implementation networks where every service is a mix of bureaucracy, markets, and civil society provides a great challenge to understanding how governance structures function. It is important to explore how the private sector which works for profit subsumes this overriding goal of its existence for the pursuit of public interest. The orientation of the private sector is that of achieving returns on invested funds, daring to take business risks, having to anticipate markets and competitive developments, and realizing a corporate goal, whereas the public sector orientation reflects political opinion and influence, formulation of legislation, regulations, and authorities, democratic decision-making process, the minimization of risk, and realization of a social goal ([Reijners 1994: 224] quoted in Datta [2009: 73–4]). Are there conflicts in working together? If yes, how are they resolved and in which direction are the bargains struck?

Rhodes (2006: 439), for example, points out that we need to be clear about what we mean when we call for effective service delivery because the criterion of effectiveness vary. The competition that characterizes the markets conflicts with cooperation that is so characteristic of networks. There has been a widespread impression that networks have been cases of privatization by 'stealth' and the bargains have been in general more favourable to corporate interests.

The strategy of pursuing PPP as a strategy of development has led to establishing new kinds of institutions that are not necessarily and not always part of government hierarchy. The fundamental concern here is that with the formation of new institutions of policymaking and delivery of services and goods, how do the various actors with divergent orientations work together to achieve the goals of efficiency and equity. What is the impact of these new institutions on the functioning of democracy and state? The issue of accountability is at the forefront of all academic and people's concerns. To whom are these partnerships accountable and how?

Who finds representation in these partnerships? Is the functioning of these partnerships transparent?

Without ignoring many of these questions, it is necessary to remind ourselves that the concept of partnership reflects empirical reality much more sharply than what focus on government alone did. It points to networks in society that are involved in policymaking and moves away from the well-established notions of authoritative single agencies at work. Networks connect disparate set of actors who jointly realize that they need one another to craft effective political agreements.

But their efforts to find solutions acceptable to all who are involved tend to challenge the constitutional institutions established for this purpose (see Hajer and Wagenaar 2003). The institutional architecture promoted by these reforms does not fall into the accountability system laid down constitutionally in a parliamentary system of government. In the quest for efficiency, the government institutions seeking partnership with the private sector are sought to be kept out of political control. Emergence of semi-autonomous institutions marks a departure from bureaucratic implementation, which was accountable to the ministers and citizens. The relationship between state and market and ensuing issues of accountability keep recurring in governance reform efforts.

A final underlying theme in the current thinking of reforming government is its thrust on depoliticizing institutions. This point we have repeatedly emphasized earlier in the setting up of semi-autonomous institutions. Public choice theory had placed its faith in the attributes of the market in providing public goods and services efficiently by painting a dismal picture of the political scene. This theme has been taken up in the thinking of new public management, as well that of governance institution designs. Thus, in this sense, PPPs are as much about ideological response to the global agenda of governance reforms as they are about managerial and technocratic innovations and institutional reforms.

8 Partnership in Policy Process
Government and Business

Partnership with the private sector as a way of 'steering' society was part of the old adage that came down from early contribution to liberal economic reforms in the thrust for reinventing the government. Private sector cooperation in framing public policy is being sought out where the long legacy of state monopoly in such matters has persisted and where a culture of suspicion of business and large corporate sector to pursue public good existed. A brief narration of the features of the state—business relationship before the introduction of economic reforms is necessary to understand the later policy developments and the challenges this strategy of implementing development programmes faces.

Soon after Independence, India chose a strategy of centralized planning where the state would occupy commanding heights and the private sector would be controlled and regulated to achieve the goals set for development. The Planning Commission was established in 1950 and given the responsibility of preparing plans that would regulate and promote economic activities according to the priorities laid down. Pursuing the goal of rational allocation of resources, plan priorities were set. A system of industrial licensing was introduced around the time of the First Five-Year Plan, which was implemented during early 1950s. This meant that companies had to seek permission from the government to establish business in specified areas. Production targets were fixed by the planners and any change in them needed their approval. To administer the industrial licensing system, a central advisory council with strong representation of private business interests was established, supplemented by separate development councils for a range of important individual industries. Private business interests were also represented in many other regulating bodies that were established during this period.

This was the time when considerable space was provided to the private sector to invest in the production of goods and services, but in areas identified in the plan. The licensing regime was relatively liberal during the Nehruvian years and the private sector investment grew more rapidly than anticipated. The government's attitude towards the private sector was flexible and pragmatic rather than rigid (Panagriya 2008: 37–40). The ideological justifications were added during the regime of Indira Gandhi. Introducing the Second Five-Year Plan in Parliament, Nehru had declared:

> May I say that while I am for public sector growing, I do not understand or appreciate the condemnation of the private sector. The whole philosophy underlying this Plan is to take advantage of every possible path of growth and not to do something which suits some doctrinaire theory or imagine we have grown because we have satisfied some text-book maxim of hundred years ago.[1]

The relations between business and government soured during the period of Nehru's successor, Indira Gandhi. New controls over industry were introduced, making the process of procuring

---

[1] In the neoliberal rhetoric in contemporary India, Nehru is criticized for giving too much role to state in economic affairs. Guha (2014: 133) calls this criticism anachronistic. Citing that the Bombay Plan framed leading industrialists in 1944, he goes on to add that most business houses wanted state to build infrastructure projects and to protect them from foreign competition. This is their demand even today.

licenses to set up new industry or expand the existing capacities more cumbersome and difficult. A vast network of administrative and regulatory institutions emerged to oversee that priorities and investment norms were followed. A system of bureaucratic controls as instruments of public policy was put in place, which led to the strengthening of the power of the civil service. Manifestation of this power was not only reflected in rigidity in applying rules, but also in attitudes of distrust and suspicion of the private sector (Mathur 2013). The period was marked by the emergence of lobby groups representing individual business houses trying to extract concessions from the government. The role of these lobby groups was to influence the government to get concessions in their favour, not to change the law (Kochanek 1996).

A kind of clandestine partnership emerged between the state and business in India. As Kochanek (1987: 1284) points out, the political leadership came to depend very heavily on the system as quid pro quo for securing campaign contributions, and the bureaucracy depended on it for payoffs, employment, power, prestige, and patronage. The business community depended on the system to secure and maintain monopoly, protection, and guaranteed profitability. In this relationship, it does not come as a surprise that among business houses the larger ones commanded more power and influence. The administration assumed powers that could have a negative impact on the fortunes of business houses and thus became a regulator and not a facilitator for business to grow. And bureaucracy did not hesitate to take advantage of this situation. A vast network of administrative institutions was established to oversee the implementation of priorities and regulate investment.

The introduction of liberal economic reforms in 1991 signalled far-reaching changes in the government's economic policies and a change in the role of the state and government. Policy and governance reforms were seen as efforts to create a favourable environment for the private sector to grow and invest in India's growth.

Unlike during the period of planning, business houses were no more seen as hostile actors out to subvert the goals of the state, but as partners in achieving them. The minister of company affairs, speaking at a seminar in 2006, emphasized that the role of the private enterprise in taking the country to higher and higher growth paths is very important. The government's role is to provide a conducive atmosphere in which business could flourish. He then went on to stress the need of freedom of action and initiative by the enterprises as against the pre-reform mindset of viewing the business and its efforts at growth and expansion with suspicion. 'We are in the era of PPP', he said.[2] This theme found sustenance in the idea of PPP, and an effort was made to search for institutional arrangements that would promote it.

The government sought alliance with big business houses in order to pursue the goal of accelerated economic growth (Kohli 2006). It began with initiating many policies that withdrew the controlling and regulating role of the state and then went on to establish institutional structures that provided a formal forum where the big businesses could participate in policymaking. Such a government–business alliance has been evolving since then, and the government has been seeking business support for achieving the goal of accelerating the rate of economic growth. The Indian administrative system is enjoined to facilitate businesses to invest by relaxing rules and changing policies.

CREATING POLICY NETWORKS

The interaction with business began to be promoted at both the individual firm level and at the collective level. There were two well-established business associations until the 1990s—the Federation of Indian Chambers of Commerce and Industry

[2] http://www.indlawnews.com/38015ad8fc90dc27e781af47f5446e2d

(FICCI) and Associated Chambers of Commerce and Industry (ASSOCHAM), which had been established before Independence. A third association that began to play a critical role in policy process emerged in 1992, the Confederation of Indian Industry (CII). In terms of formal policy role, business associations participated in consultative capacity in many forums such as government committees and advisory groups. At the highest level, with the prime minister as chair, the Council on Trade and Industry was created as an institutional framework for policy consultations between government and business. The prime minister emphasized that creating such a network flows from our overall strategy of economic reforms.

This council was appointed with a notification in 1998 and this practice has continued with the change of governments in 2004 and 2009 too. The council provided an opportunity for a policy dialogue on important economic issues relevant to trade and industry between the prime minister and members of the council. The council ordinarily met once in three months on such dates as decided by its chairman. The membership of the council nearly doubled—from 10 to 18 members—between the years the governments changed, incorporating many more industrialists rising on the economic horizon. In addition, special subgroups were also appointed to interact directly with ministries. Such subgroups were appointed in areas such as food and agro–industries, management policy, infrastructure, capital markets and financial sector initiatives, knowledge-based industries, service industries, and administrative and legal simplifications.

This institutional architecture has not received much attention from the government that was elected in 2014. While consultations with business leaders continue, a formal system of their participation in public policy process does not seem to have emerged.

However, this was the period when individuals with a background in senior policy positions with the private sector were inducted in policy spaces in the government. In 2009, the Planning Commission opened its doors to one such person who had worked with business houses Tata Motors and Arthur D. Little and was senior advisor with Boston Consulting Group. In another decision co-chairman of Infosys Technologies and a leading spokesman for information technology industry was appointed chairman of Unique Identification Authority of India with the rank of a minister of state.

What is significant about the membership of these councils (1998–2014) is that trade unions/labour federations and NGOs go unrepresented. It is presumed that gains in the rate of economic growth or relaxing of government norms is a technical problem and can be decided within an expert body and those who can invest. Part of the effort is also to insulate economic decision-making from the political process. In Britain, a three-way partnership was institutionalized in the National Economic Development Council launched in 1962. During the 1980s, the council diminished in its significance and met infrequently. The prime minister, Thatcher, was of the opinion that trade unions had no legitimate role in policymaking and should, therefore, be excluded. The council was finally disbanded in 1992 (Dorey 2005: 125).

The government that came to power in 2014 has charted a different path of bringing the private sector into public policy spaces. It is strongly influenced by the personal style of leadership of the prime minister, Narendra Modi. As chief minister of Gujarat, he had developed robust connections with business houses organizing vibrant Gujarat summits. The first such summit was organized in 2003 when a 1,000 participants with 230 foreign delegates attended it. The numbers continued to rise in later summits with increasing commitments of investment in the state. This gave him a public celebration of being a developmental man.

As prime minister, he mobilized private sector support through the slogan of 'Make in India'. He has appealed to business entrepreneurs and leaders to work as a team with the government to make India prosperous. In his inimitable style, he has been meeting business leaders in India and abroad, assuring them of a congenial business climate. In 2017, he held a meeting with 212 start-up founders and young entrepreneurs and later met a large number of CEOs, seeking policy inputs. In order to be more focused in their recommendations, CEOs have worked in groups on specific themes. These groups are tasked to formulate strategies on certain topics. These groups may be attached to ministries as part of an institutionalizing process to ensure that they act as guiding lights to crucial issues (see *Economic Times* 14 September 2017).

These meetings are attended by cabinet ministers and senior bureaucrats. From what we saw from the preceding discussion, the networks tend to blur the boundaries of public and private interests. In participative decision-making, it is the large corporations that exercise vast economic and social power. They have greater opportunities to push their own agendas and take advantage of this fuzziness as a weak and demoralized bureaucracy is being constantly berated for not playing an enabling role adequately. In any case, the bureaucracy itself is being exposed to corporate goals and practices through changed rules of deputation and service rules.

It is important to note, however, that the entry of the private sector into the public policy institutional space is making the collaboration between the government and business more open and transparent; the era of clandestine lobbying is receding into the past. But the network governance also obscures the process and accountability for public policy formulation, decision-making, and execution. It opens the door to involvement by a wider range of actors in ways that are less constrained than those applying to institutional political authority (Mathur and Skelcher 2007: 235).

The policy impact of such networks on socially and economically deprived groups leads to their exclusion and not to the prophesized benefits from the market. The private sector is hesitant to partner with the government's non-profit schemes. For example, when the government promotes a PPP to structure the urban water supply scheme, it excludes those who cannot pay for water; it is, in a very real way, abdicating its own responsibilities. Or say, primary education and primary health care suffer at the cost of market-responsive technical education or highly sophisticated speciality hospitals.

9 Public–Private Partnership (PPP) as an Administrative Institution

As business houses began to be incorporated in policy and advisory bodies, new institutions began to be established to implement development programmes. If it was a new role for the state, business was also carving out a new role for itself. It was no longer an agency reacting to government policy, but was now actively involved in framing that policy. It was also now in a position to influence the choice of areas of investment and, once having been chosen, demand the kind of facilitation it needed from government to invest.

As an institution for implementing development programmes, PPP has taken many forms and has become amenable to many definitions. Lakshmanan (2008) points out that there is no internationally agreed definition of a PPP. While it is broadly agreed that PPP is transfer of private investment to infrastructure projects that were traditionally in the realm of the public sector, the form that it takes is in the realm of ambiguity. The PPP may encompass the whole spectrum of approaches, from private participation through contracting out services and revenue sharing partnership arrangement to pure non-recourse project finance, while sometimes it may include only a narrow range of project type. The PPP has two important characteristics. First, there is an emphasis on service provision as well as investment by the private sector. Second, significant risk is transferred from the government to the private sector. The PPP model is very flexible and discernible in a variety of forms (Lakksmanan 2008: 40).

There are diverse modalities of establishing PPPs. First, it can be an institution where the private sector designs, builds, owns, develops, operates, and manages an asset with no obligation to transfer ownership to the government. These are variants of design-build-finance-operate (DBFO) schemes. Second, the private sector buys or leases an existing asset from the government, renovates, modernizes, and/or expands it, and then operates the asset, again with no obligation to transfer ownership back to the government. In another variant, the private sector designs and builds an asset, operates it, and then transfers it to the government when the operating contract ends or at some other pre-specified time. The private partner may subsequently rent or lease the asset from the government.

The Government of India in *PPP Guide for Practitioners* has put forward a definition of PPP based on thinking on PPPs in countries such as UK, South Africa, and Australia (Government of India 2016). It says that these countries view PPPs as an alternate form of public procurement whereby public infrastructure and/or public services are procured through the private sector. They treat efficient delivery of services as the key drivers of PPP as opposed to merely substituting private investment for public capital expenditure. Efficient delivery of services, in turn, is achieved by substantial transfer of risk to the private sector and remuneration being based on outputs achieved by the private sector. The key is to harness the private sector's private motive by incentivizing it to provide better quality service and earn a reasonable return (Government of India 2008: 6).

The Government of India then provides for an all-inclusive definition when it says that PPPs are an arrangement between a government or statutory entity or government-owned entity, on one side, and a private-sector entity, on the other, for the provision of public assets and/or related services for public benefit, through investments being made by and/or management undertaken by the private sector entity for a specified time period, where there is a substantial risk sharing with the private sector. The private sector receives performance-linked payments that conform (or are benchmarked) to specified, predetermined, and measurable performance standards.

There is a general agreement that following are characteristics of a successful PPP project. These are:

1. Allocation of risks in an optimal manner: the PPP models should have a sensible model of sharing of responsibilities, cost, and risk. 'Assignment of risk is the principle that needs to be adopted.'
2. Performance-linked fee payment
3. Term of the contract depends on the kind of job to be undertaken
4. Incentive- and penalty-based structures
5. Outcomes of the PPP are normally predefined as output parameters
6. There are formal contracts or a memorandum of understanding defining the role and obligations of each partner

Leaving it open for different government authorities to define PPP means that the concept has become flexible to suit the needs of a particular agency. The result of such flexibility is that little distinction is made between outsourcing and partnership. In the variants of the DBFO scheme, there is no obligation to transfer the asset created to the government. Thus, such a scheme can also be called partnership. The period of the partnership is also not specified, which leaves open the issue of ambiguity.

The most important aspect is that there is a formal legal contract that lays down the obligations of the partners and the way revenue will be shared. Where large finance is involved, banks and financial institutions also play an important role in determining the way revenue sharing will take place. The PPP is established as a semi-autonomous institution in which the contract is laid down.

INSTITUTIONAL SUPPORT FOR PROMOTING PPPs

The government has taken several steps to accelerate the process of investment and remove impediments. As a sign of importance attached to this strategy, a committee on infrastructure was established in 2004 under the chairmanship of the prime minister, as the infrastructure demands the highest volume of investment. In 2009, this committee was converted into the Cabinet Committee for Infrastructure Projects chaired by the prime minister. A PPP cell was established in the Ministry of Finance to support a coherent policy framework. Together with this, nodal officers of the rank of joint secretaries were appointed in relevant ministries to expedite approvals. States were also encouraged to appoint such nodal officers.

A key initiative of the government to promote PPPs is the Viability Gap Funding scheme. This is meant to provide financial support to those infrastructure projects that are economically justifiable but are not commercially viable. In the eligible list of projects, those in the urban and in the tourism sector are included apart from the ones in sectors such as road, airports, and so on. The eligibility list includes projects in urban transport, water supply, sewerage, solid waste management, and other physical infrastructure in urban areas. Such projects will be eligible for a grant of 20 per cent of the total cost of the project. India Infrastructure Finance Company has been set up with the specific mandate to play a catalytic role in the infrastructure sector by providing long-term debt for financing infrastructure projects.

ORIENTING CIVIL SERVANTS

Recognizing that the Indian administrators were nurtured in a policy environment of state intervention for public good, the government initiated several measures to reorient them to the new tasks of facilitating private sector to invest in development projects and be their partners and not their regulators. Rules for interaction with business were relaxed, and India more actively sought the support of Asian Development Bank (ADB) in conducting regional workshops for state civil servants as part of its effort to mainstream PPPs in India. Representatives of the private sector also participated in these workshops, for the aim was also to present their key concerns. In 2006, the Department of Economic Affairs (DEA), Ministry of Finance, Government of India, and ADB organized four Regional Workshops of Chief Secretaries on Public–Private Partnership (PPP) for Accelerated Infrastructure Development in India. The workshops were held between June and September 2006 in Bengaluru, Delhi, Kolkata, and Goa (ADB 2006).

The government has been keen to expose civil servants to the practices in the private sector and attune them to the liberal perspective. Training programmes have a component of visits to countries that have successfully implemented privatization programmes. But it has clamped down on its earlier service rule that allowed them to work in a private sector organization during their government tenure. The Second Administrative Reforms Commission's 10th report on personnel administration mentions that this prohibition was inserted in the service rules in 2007 after it was apprehended that such deputation to private sector organizations and financial companies may lead to conflict-of-interest situations. The commission recognized that the government and the private sector espouse different values, work culture, and managerial practices. Public sector promotes commitment to public service, equality, and justice while the private sector brings modern management practices, innovations, flexibility, and absence of red-tapism. Taking these factors into consideration, the commission has recommended deputation should be permitted to only such organizations that are engaged in non-profit activities (Second Administrative Reforms Commission 2008: 215).

It appears significant that the government recognizes that the prevailing administrative system is not adequately responsive to the demands of a liberal economy. It has been bred on regulating and enforcing rules on the way the private sector conducts itself. This is very different from facilitating it to do business. It is also significant that the World Bank and ADB play an important role in influencing policies of PPPs in India and reorient civil servants' perspectives towards the private sector. The emerging style of governance emphasized an 'enabling' state whose role was to create conditions in which private investment could take place.[1]

Recognizing that the potential of PPPs is not being realized in the education and health sector, ADB, in pursuing its mandate of 'mainstreaming PPPs in India', has brought out several sector-related papers delineating policy directions and models of financing implementation of projects. It engaged KPMG (a global consultancy firm), on behalf of the DEA, Ministry of Finance, Government of India, to develop possible solutions to meet the challenges in the primary health care and primary education (primary and upper-primary schools) sectors in the country through the use of PPP modalities. In the field of health care, the document offers the following three models: (*i*) primary healthcare centre—adoption, management contracts, and mobile clinics; (*ii*) for diagnostic services, build, own, and operate model; and (*iii*) for building infrastructure, Hospital Private Finance Initiative (PFI) Scheme. In the field of education, the policy direction for improving the quality of teaching is management contracts, mentoring programmes, teacher supply and training, and information and communications technology training centres. For maintaining school buildings, the model is that of build, lease, and maintain school buildings, and provision of schools in rural areas is also through PPP (Mehta, Bhatia, and

---

[1] In fact, the World Bank conducts a worldwide survey assessing the business environment and the speed with which the government responds to an application to set up an enterprise. India has been usually ranked low in the past many years.

Chatterjee 2010). Similar policy papers have also been prepared in the fields of water supply, sanitation, and so on.

EMERGING ISSUES

The enthusiasm for PPPs as a strategy of implementing development programmes is great and is receiving wide support from liberal-minded policymakers. The prime minister has made public pronouncements supporting the strategy and it has been incorporated as a strategy of implementation in the 11th and 12th Five-Year Plans. The changed government in 2014 has added its own enthusiasm to this strategy. What began as a mode of developing physical infrastructure now embraces the gambit of all kinds of services that lay earlier in government domain. According to the Government of India website, around 758 PPP projects being implemented or are underway across the country. The total project cost is estimated to be about ₹38,333,206 crores (1 crore equals 1,000,000). Among the states, the leading users have been Karnataka, Andhra Pradesh, and Madhya Pradesh. The road projects account for 54.3 per cent of the total number of projects and 46 per cent of the total value. The report points out that the potential use of PPPs in e-governance, education, and health remains largely untapped across India as a whole. There are increasing investments taking place in urban development, and the value of contracts as of 31 July 2011 stands at ₹29,475 crores with 152 projects.

A 2016 study by ASSOCHAM reports that a total of 1,200 projects in different segments of infrastructure with investments worth ₹7,00,000 crore are being carried throughout the country. Of these, the major share of projects and investments is in roads and bridges followed by those in ports and energy.[2]

---

[2] See www.assocham.org/newsdetail.php?id=5634, last accessed on 8 October 2017.

Whatever the sense of achievement the above-mentioned figures may show, the extent of private sector investment in PPP projects did not occur as expected and many projects were stalled due to various reasons. In the budget speech for the year 2015–16, the finance minister, however, reiterated the government's enthusiasm for pursuing the PPP mode of infrastructural development. A committee under the chairmanship of Vijay Kelkar was set up in 2015 to suggest ways to revitalize the effort. Reporting towards the end of the year, the committee made several recommendations that would facilitate investment and attract private capital. Emphasizing that PPPs in infrastructure are a valuable instrument of development and also that India is the world's largest market for PPPs, the committee urged the need to build institutional capacities. It referred to changing mindsets and recommended structured capacity-building programmes for different stakeholders including implementing agencies. The committee also recommended a dispute-resolution mechanism, regulatory agency, facilitation in writing contracts, and so on (Government of India 2015a).

There appears to be a sense of urgency in accelerating the pace of PPPization in India as demonstrated by rapid publication of enabling conditions and establishing approval mechanisms at the highest levels. There is a push by international development agencies, as PPP is central to their development strategy. Much of the foreign direct investments (FDI) and loans being made available by the World Bank or the ADB are premised on the assumption that projects will be implemented in the PPP mode whether they are in the infrastructure or social sector. For the private sector, PPPs in infrastructure are opportunities for heavy investment, windows for entering a market that is very large, and a market space to stay for a long period of time. The government finds this partnership bringing in finances and world-class technology, and so partnerships seem to have worked in the infrastructure sector. However, projects have yet to be evaluated for efficiency, costs, and adoption of latest technology.

In the social sector, private investment, particularly FDI, presents another significant issue that challenges the public service orientation of public administration. As the private sector is concerned about profits and comes into partnership only if these are forthcoming, it tends to get concentrated in regions and sectors where profits are assured. In the case of hospitals, for example, in most of the states, private investment has remained an urban phenomenon. This reflects that income—based on people's ability to pay—serves as a major magnet for attracting corporate players in hospital sector (Hooda 2015: 13).

As a project implementation unit, PPP is established as a semi-autonomous unit set apart from a ministry or part of its hierarchy. The most significant part of its establishment is the nature of contract that is signed between the government and business entity. This contract determines the sharing of risks, pooling of resources, and the way the costs of the project are to be borne. User fees and the term of the project are also important considerations.

Partnership is based on equality, but in the real world the government and business may not turn out to be equal partners. The strength of the private sector lies in its ability to not participate in any project that does not assure it adequate returns (read profits). This leaves little option to the government other than diluting its contractual advantages to fulfill its demands. Over the years, suspicion has grown that in this weak–strong relationship, private partners have used their strength to leverage more favourable terms for themselves.[3]

What is significant in the structure of support system to encourage the states to promote PPP projects is that there is no mention of

---

[3] Evidence of this can be seen in Delhi government's construction of two super-specialty hospitals and soliciting private partners to manage them. In spite of its efforts, tender announcements, and shortlisting, the government could not find a partner (see Mathur et al. 2012).

any mechanism for evaluation of projects. The government does not provide itself any window of learning about the way partnerships are formed and contracts written up. It depends on the inputs provided by funding agencies and the private sector through what have come to be known as creating a knowledge domain. There is no way of evaluating whether a project under PPP has been more efficiently or economically implemented than if it was under government. The profit drive of the private sector should be leveraged for the public good and not for profiteering. One reason some private entities shy away from public disclosure could be that the revenue models are heavily skewed in their favour. It could be through corruption, or just inexperience and inefficiency on the part of government officials in drafting proper pacts (Sebastian 2011).

As Bagal (2008) points out, 'If governments are to handle a large number of PPP projects, then they have to start developing the necessary manpower and groups of skilled, knowledgeable and dedicated functionaries.' The major weakness in successfully implementing PPP projects lies in design and terms of contracts. The government functionaries lack the expertise to counter the bargaining expertise of large corporates. Kelkar Committee, established to review the performance of PPPs, endorses this view. The committee goes on to further add that success requires change in the mindset of all authorities dealing with PPPs and building their capacity.

However, investment in PPPs continues unabated, despite the lack of evidence that they work well.[4] Enthusiasm for PPPs is going to extreme lengths when the Rajasthan government announces its tie-up with the corporate sector's Future Group to manage the

---

[4] It is reported from data up to 2016 that a total of 1,200 projects in different segments of infrastructure sector with investments worth 7 lakh crore rupees are being carried out throughout India. Of the major share in projects and investments is in roads and bridges followed by those in ports and energy. See www.aasocham.org/newsdetail.php?id=5634, accessed on 10 October 2017.

overall public distribution system. Its public distribution system (PDS) and ration shops will undergo a facelift and be branded as Annapurna Bhandar (*Economic Times* 21 August 2015). The PDS has specially been designed and implemented to serve the poor and those who cannot avail of the market. It is yet to be seen how this partnership can serve these values of public interest.

10 Provisioning of Education and Health in Public–Private Partnership (PPP) Mode

Public–Private Partnerships (PPPs) began with infrastructure projects as these demanded heavy investments, which only the private sector could provide. Now they are being tried in the social sector. While the challenge that policymakers face in the infrastructure sector is that of creating a more favourable, enabling state to attract greater private investment, the story of PPP projects in the social sector has an additional challenge. The concern is not only of creating physical infrastructure but also of providing access to it equitably. With these concerns in mind or by ignoring them, the government is moving towards different forms of PPPs at various education levels. There are frequent announcements that the government is establishing more schools in this mode. Sometime back, an erstwhile HRD minister announced that the government was planning to set up over 2,500 model and 200 central schools on PPP basis in the country in the next two years (*Indian Express* 29 August 2009). He added that the schools would be set up in PPP as part of their efforts to strengthen human resource base and then went on to ask the corporate houses to invest in a big way in the education sector, emphasizing that developing human resources is key to the success of any nation.

Other institutions and researchers have also joined in stressing the need of introducing PPPs in the education sector for similar reasons and also for fulfilling the commitment of raising literacy levels. A World Bank study (Jagannathan 2001) has explored the working of six NGOs that extend primary education to rural children in India. It argued that these NGOs have demonstrated effective grassroots action to enhance the quality of basic education and have also influenced mainstream education through replication of their models and through policy dialogue with the government. While suggesting that NGOs are best suited for small projects and micro-level interventions, the study strongly advocates sustainable and enduring partnership with the voluntary sector which will strengthen the government's efforts to actualize the goal of universal elementary education. In their official documents both the World Bank as well as ADB have been advocating the policy of 'pppization'.

Centre for Civil Society launched a School Choice Campaign in 2007, arguing that what the poor need today 'is not just Right to Education, but the Right to Education of Choice'. It advocates PPP through the use of voucher system. It carries on a policy campaign advocating quality education by providing choices to the poor. This can be done through a voucher system in which students are funded not schools.[1] The Ambani–Birla Committee, appointed by Prime Minister's Council of Trade and Industry, went on to recommend in its report in 2000 that there needs to be greater association of the private sector in higher education.[2] FICCI has been holding summits in higher education from 2004. It has been organizing them as annual international events with the

[1] Centre for Civil Society has been carrying policy campaign through presentations in seminars and conferences advocating right to school choice through voucher system. See its website, http://schoolchoice.in/aboutus/ccs.php.

[2] 'Policy Framework for Reform in Education', available at ispepune.in/PDF Issue/2003/JISPE403/2038DOCU-3PDF.

support of Ministry of Human Resources Development and the Planning Commission, Government of India. For sometime now, Ernst and Young has joined FICCI to prepare the background paper in these meetings. In the paper prepared for the 2009 summit, titled 'Leveraging Partnerships in India in Education Sector', the need for PPPs in higher education sector is underlined. This is necessary to meet the financial constraints of the government and to meet the demand of skilled persons of the industry. It identifies various types of partnerships and also recommends collaboration with foreign universities for research and student exchange.[3]

Thus, the international donor agencies, corporate houses, and some civil society organizations are demanding greater PPP in the education sector. The government having articulated its commitment to provide education for all through the enactment of the Right to Education into law is also becoming receptive to these ideas, for it is facing a resource crunch and lack of capacity to run a responsive and efficient educational system.

But having articulated its commitment to PPPs in education, the government is still at the stage of experimentation. For one thing, the forms that partnerships can take in education are diverse. Government aid to schools is a form of partnership that has existed from a long time, but does not fit into the current mould. In this partnership, a private entrepreneur or trust provided the school buildings and infrastructure while the government paid for the salary of teachers and regulated the curriculum and quality of teaching. There are also alternatives where the government just provides the land and infrastructural facilities at varying rates of subsidy. There are now many other openings such as financing of services like those of IT, underwriting mid-day meals, or handing

---

[3] See report at www.ey.com/Publication/vwLUAssets/Private_sector_participation_in_Indian_higher_education/$FILE/Private_sector_participation_in_Indian_higher_education.pdf.

over of a school to the private sector to provide management services.

At the level of higher education, the forms it can take is in establishing research collaboration between government and industry, giving space to private entrepreneurs to enter the field, and opening up for partnership with foreign universities. For quite some time, large business houses have been a big player in the field of higher education such as engineering and medical education. These institutions were primarily colleges affiliated to universities which exercised control over their academic norms. These colleges were seen as a response to the market's need for more professionals as doctors and technologists. By the mid-1990s, promoters of private colleges saw the regulatory control of the affiliating university and state governments as cumbersome, impeding the full utilization of the colleges' market potential. Thus, they wanted university status to wriggle out of the control of state governments and the affiliating universities. This resulted in the proliferation of private universities and private-deemed universities. Earlier, the deemed university provision that empowered an institution to award its own degree was sparingly used to allow leading institutions to offer programmes at an advanced level in a particular field or specialization. The Indian Institute of Science in Bangalore and the Indian Agricultural Research Institute in Delhi were the first two institutions to be declared deemed universities in 1958. This number increased to 29 in 1990/91 and 38 in 1998 and as of 2017 stands at 129. Most of the post-1998 deemed universities are private.[4] The current minister of

---

[4] The sector of higher education has witnessed a tremendous increase in the number of universities/university level institutions since Independence. The number of universities has increased 34 times from 20 in 1950 to 677 in 2014. There are 45 central universities, 318 state run, 185 private universities, 129 deemed to be universities, and 51 institutes of national importance (see mhrd.gov.in/university-and-higher-education).

HRD is soliciting partnerships with universities in USA and UK to enhance the quality of education in India.

Privatization in higher education went apace with greater adherence to the governance model laid out in the neoliberal framework. Colleges providing professional education in engineering and medicine and schools at secondary and higher secondary levels multiplied in the private sector. Private sector was hesitant to enter primary schooling for it perceived that it did not give adequate dividends. But even its entry at the level of professional colleges has not at all been a success story. A recent announcement by the chairperson of All India Council Technical Education (AICTE) says that 800 engineering colleges that have had a student enrollment of less than 30 per cent over 5 years will be shut down from the coming academic year. However, keeping up with the broader context of neoliberalism, an official from the same council also says that there is no need for the AICTE to intervene and close down colleges. These colleges will eventually shut down when there is no market demand (*The Hindu* 2 September 2017).

In the past four decades, the number of universities has grown more than six times. One-third of 33,023 colleges have been set up only during the past five years. The number of private institutions have grown faster than public institutions (Gupta 2015: 360). Some of these institutions are now vigorously seeking alliance with foreign universities to enhance their credibility. The current government is actively encouraging this outreach, for this provides the ladder to compete with international institutions and have a place in world rankings.

Privatization has also meant that these institutions are out of the government's direct control. For this reason, they have been loosely regulated by it. In any case, there are some regulatory bodies such as the University Grants Commission (UGC) and AICTE and some professional councils. Many professional institutions are directly under relevant ministries that finance and regulate them.

For-profit organizations, however, have entered for personal gain, introducing unscrupulous practices that seem to exploit the students and the community. These practices are not only related to what is taught and how, but also to financial misdemeanors. There are now capitation-fee colleges which demand high admission fees, and the students are asked to bear the costs of services that may be advertised but not provided. There is now an increasing risk that financial costs and fees may be out of the reach of a vast number of students and may lead to restricting education to those who have the ability to pay. Economic deprivation may also result in educational deprivation.

Another equally important, if not more, aspect is the fear that for-profit institutions and foreign collaborations may not fulfill India's quest for social equity. Broadening access may leave out the socially deprived segment of the population. Policies of affirmative action have been pursued in government institutions, while private institutions are not mandated to do so. Such expansion in education may not fulfill social aspirations unless adequate steps are taken. Recent surveys and data alert us to what the future may hold.

For example, in Delhi the traditional mode of providing land and infrastructural facilities at subsidized rates has dominated the scene of school education to attract the private sector. But within this sector, primary schools have not been so attractive to the private sector. Therefore, this responsibility lies with the municipality and Delhi administration. After the passage of the Right to Education Act, the Supreme Court has made it mandatory for private unaided schools to admit 25 per cent of its students from the economically weaker sections. Delhi administration has begun enforcing this mandate but has not been very successful. This insistence has met with reluctance as well as some form of resistance from many private managements of schools.

The government has turned to establishing regulatory bodies that can play a more effective role in seeing that private institutions fulfill social goals and work in an ethical fashion. At the same time, they also allow them adequate autonomy to function well. But it is still struggling to develop an appropriate design. In 2010, the then government had introduced several bills in Parliament to regulate higher educational institutions. Most of them lapsed with the coming of the new government in 2014. These bills could not be passed due to stiff resistance from the votaries of both public and private sectors. Meanwhile, the government is going ahead in its attempt to open the education sector to privatization and international higher education institutions.

Government strategy of reforming provisioning health services through PPP bears a dismal record. But in spite of apparent failures, it continues to rely on the strategy to improve people's access to health services. It is reported that even the two private parties who were part of NITI Aayog consultations for PPP in health care, the CII and the private health care federation called NATHEALTH, were hard-pressed to give examples of successful PPP in health care (*Times of India* 4 August 2017).

State governments in India, under whose jurisdiction the health sector falls, are experimenting with partnerships in many dimensions of health sector. The scope of these initiatives span disease surveillance, purchase and distribution of drugs in bulk, contracting specialists for high-risk pregnancies, national disease control programmes, social marketing, adoption and management of primary health centres, co-location of private facilities (blood banks, pharmacies), looking into subsidies and duty exemptions and joint ventures, contracting out medical education and training, engaging private sector consultants and pay clinics, and so on (Venkatraman and Bjorkman 2009: 81). It is probably because of this complexity that PPP advocates claim their inability to find successful examples.

There is no single model of partnership in health care. What is referred to as non-government sector comprises several types of medical traditions that range from local therapies to traditional medicines. Then there is allopathy, practised by individual doctors and practitioners of medicine in private clinics and nursing homes, as well as large number of super speciality hospitals. In this complex space, the government has sought partnerships with 'for-profit' private sector that usually runs larger hospitals and technical services.

In the past few years, PPPs have multiplied and have entered more fields of health care. What is significant is that in most of these PPPs, user charges have emerged for primary health care services in the urban areas, particularly where collaboration is with the private sector. The assumption is that urbanites have the capacity to pay. Thus, entry of the private sector provides little assurance to the poor for adequate health service. This is in face of the well-known fact that a large number of such hospitalized patients have to borrow money or sell assets and many fall below the poverty line to cover expenses. Thus, the dilemma is that while the public sector does not provide adequate health services, demanding services from the private sector is so expensive that it leaves them further impoverished.

Taking into account the provision of poor health services in the country, the Government of India announced the New Health Policy in 2017. The policy continues to advocate a positive engagement with the private sector and pushes for financial and non-financial incentives for it to participate in the provision of health services. NITI Aayog has also come up with a strong recommendation for increased private sector participation and has gone to the extent of proposing its participation in district hospitals in tier 2 and 3 cities. A former union health secretary has gone public criticizing the proposal and arguing that it will have adverse implications for the working of district hospitals, which are a refuge for the poor (*Indian Express* 11 August 2017). The proposal is designed to allow private sector in the infrastructure facilities to provide treatment for three diseases—cardiology, cancer, and pulmonology—while the government wing takes care of other diseases. The union health secretary has called this hybrid model 'bizarre or hair brained depending on which side of the equation one is on'.

Thus, PPP in health services is on an uncharted path of providing services to the middle and upper classes while depriving the vast majority of the poor of them. But the experience has not been a happy one even in those cases where PPP format was used to establish super specialty hospitals. Costing and pricing of services continue to worry the patients, and the government faces challenges in regulating them. While there are many examples of relative successes of PPPs in infrastructure, evidence of success in the health sector is rather limited. A health ministry official is quoted as saying: 'We have to deal with a highly corrupt private health care sector looking to maximize profits and trying to get the most out of the PPP and a government that behaves like a demanding and suspicious husband in the partnership, making impractical demands with no real management structures' (*Times of India* 4 August 2017).

Resource deficiency is cited as the reason for the government to seek partnerships in providing health care. But it appears to be a weak alibi because the government does not increase its spending on health. The recent Economic Survey 2016–17 presented to the Parliament points out that the country's public spending on health is a little over 1 per cent of GDP. It further adds that it was as low as 0.22 per cent of GDP in 1950–1 and does not seem to have made significant progress since then. The New Health Policy 2017 claims to move towards a target of 2.5 per cent, but that has been a moving target for years. It also mentions that capacity, delivery of essential services such as health and education, which are predominantly the preserve of state government, remains 'impaired'. Again, poor management of government hospitals and health centres is a reflection of lack of concern and not merely lack of finances.

If 'partnerships' have to be equitable and accountable, they need an interventionist state which can or will be willing to mediate and use its institutional, financial, and regulatory resources to create a level playing field. However, if the state itself turns out to be the enabler of market only, then such an interventionist role is doubtful. Partnerships by their very nature mean equality of partners, but over the years it has emerged that the corporate houses have used their financial and managerial strength to leverage greater advantages for themselves. Clearly, the strength of the corporate sector lies in its ability to refuse to participate in a venture that is not profitable to it.

Enthusiasm for PPPs continues, possibly because a large number of them are funded by large corporates and international donors who bring to bear their own influence on the government. Undoubtedly, PPP projects bring in capital and technology so needed by government, but policy needs to discriminate between sectors and identify those that are decisively government responsibilities. Further, it is not clear who is accountable for the projects and there is nothing to inform the concerned citizen about their impact, except what the organizations themselves choose to report. The need for comprehensive review of these projects cannot be overemphasized (Ravindran 2011: 52). It is to these questions of accountability that we turn to in the next chapter.

The challenge of introducing PPPs in education and health sectors is that of provisioning services with equity and justice. It needs no reminding that private sector enters a project with profit in view, and when the same is not on the horizon seeks many guarantees and concessions from the government to make the project viable. We have already mentioned earlier how private schools find ways to go around the provision of admitting children from economically weaker sections of society. The stories of such contracts floundering in the health sector are also being reported. A PPP was struck between a large corporate hospital in Delhi and the Delhi government, which gave 15 acres of land free of cost and made an investment of ₹23 crores with the understanding that 33 per cent of beds would be free for the deprived sections of citizens. When the Delhi government went to Court because free treatment was not being offered, it was argued that 'free bed did not mean free treatment' (*Times of India* 4 August 2017).

What must be recognized is that PPPs in the social sector and in the infrastructure sector have different characteristics. By and large, delivering public goods and services has been the prime responsibility of public administration with its ethos of public service. Assuming that the private administration will carry the same ethos is, at best, misleading in understanding its purpose.

11 Emerging Institutions and the Challenge of Democratic Accountability

New institutions that are being established rapidly to make delivery of public services and goods more efficient through the varying strategy of privatization bring in another set of challenges. In a parliamentary democracy, these challenges come in the form of accountability issues. How is the delivery accountable? To whom is it accountable?

In the traditional administrative system, clear lines of accountability were drawn. The minister was accountable to Parliament for all decisions and actions for her ministry, and Parliament consisted of elected representatives of people. This accountability was reflected in minor to major actions of the ministry. It was carried to the extent that a railway minister had held himself responsible for a railway accident and resigned from his post. His resignation had been accepted.

Parliament, in this sense, was supreme and held the minister responsible for even an act not ostensibly committed by the minister as an individual but seen as a failure of the department in his charge. Pursuit of accountability appears to be central to any democratic system, and financial accountability is its single most dimension. It is a common feature all over the world that all money owed to the government is deposited in a designated fund and no expenditure from this fund can be made without the authorization of Parliament.

It is natural then that Parliament needs to know how the authorized expenditure has been made and whether it was done for the purpose laid down by it. There are innumerable transactions and many government institutions that spend the money. A special office is usually created to fulfill the role of auditing these expenditures made through multiple transactions and institutions.

An institution with constitutional mandate that helps Parliament to hold the executive accountable to it is the office of the comptroller and auditor general (CAG). The CAG of India is appointed under Article 148 of India's Constitution and holds office for five years. In order to give him independence from the government, his terms and conditions are laid down in three further Articles. This independence or autonomy is an integral part of his ability to audit government expenditures without fear or favour of the government of the day. The Constitution laid down that the scope of his duties and functions would be left to Parliament to frame.

An Act detailing the duties and powers of the CAG was passed by Parliament in 1971. Apart from maintaining government accounts, the CAG has been mandated to audit (*i*) all expenditure from the Consolidated Fund of India, (*ii*) all transactions of the Union and all states relating to Contingency Fund and Public Accounts, and (*iii*) all trading, manufacturing, and profit and loss accounts and balance sheets and other subsidiary kept in any department. Following these sections of the Act, the CAG is empowered to audit accounts of anybody that receives grants and loans from the government. However, the CAG can be relieved of his duties of audit in cases where the president thinks it would be in public interest.

While the first 20 years of the existence of the office were spent in debating the scope of his functions and duties with A.K. Chanda, who was CAG in the latter half of 1950s and was a major contributor, the actual legal mandate was established only with the passage of the Act in 1971. The challenges that the CAG faces in defining his scope of activities, particularly after liberalization, is due to the ability of the executive to define, expand, or limit his mandate, which the Constitution has delegated it to do. With Parliament, as we shall see, remaining by and large indifferent to the role of CAG in holding the government accountable, government's discretion remains an unseen challenge.

The CAG presents his reports to the Public Accounts Committee of the Parliament and is accountable to it. Further action on these reports is taken by the committee on behalf of Parliament.

The mandate given by the Act has been all encompassing, and the CAG, as asserted by Kaul, has been reviewing government schemes and programmes and commenting on the economy, efficiency, and effectiveness of these programmes both on the expenditure and receipts side (2012: 38). Recently, however, some questions about the scope of the mandate have been raised. The prime minister, speaking to some editors on 29 June 2012, stated: 'It is not the CAG's business to comment on policy issues. I think they should limit themselves to the mandate given under the Constitution.' This issue has risen particularly in the case of what is known as performance auditing where, as another former CAG contends, 'the auditor goes beyond the mere accounting of expenditure and examines the wisdom behind the decision to spend and also whether policy objectives were met' (Shunglu 2012: 21).

Shunglu (2012: 22) gives two examples to support his contention. One is that of performance of a primary health centre where the auditor can raise questions about the performance of the doctor to see whether the functions he was expected to perform have been performed wholly or in part. He takes up the audit of the Mid-Day Meal Scheme as another example. There are many alternatives in delivering food to the children, from distributing food grains to children to pre-cooked food to fresh cooked food. It is the duty of the auditor to comment on the alternative that best fulfills the objective of the policy. The issue of mandate and scope continues to be debated with reference to the new governance institutions, as we shall see later.

This debate continues but the political impact of certain audit reports of the CAG that had commented on the role of ministers in power has been significant in recent times. The CAG has raised major issues of corruption that have had an impact on the political fortunes of parties in power at the time. Such indictments have brought the office into controversy. It is in this regard that the issue of bias and partisanship of CAG has been raised. From 1948 to the present, there have been around a dozen CAGs, and all of them have come from the IAS. These have been individuals who have served in senior and important administrative positions and have been given the responsibility of auditing many a time the agencies over which they presided. CAG, being a constitutional position, not only commands considerable prestige, but also perks of office. The tenure is also for 6 years or more up to the age of 65. It is natural for eligible IAS officers to aspire for such a position after retirement from government jobs and also to prepare themselves to be found suitable for it. This suitability can be in developing partisan relations with the powers which may be influential in such appointments.

In 2012, the leader of the opposition in Parliament, L.K. Advani, had written to the prime minister to constitute a broad-based collegium to appoint the chief election commissioner and CAG. He argued that such appointments do not evoke public confidence because the present system was vulnerable to manipulation and partisanship. Former CAG V.N. Shunglu, in his report on the Commonwealth Games controversies, had suggested that the work of CAG now undertaken by an individual should be performed by a multi-member body. Several voices from political parties also joined this refrain but the government rejected the suggestion on the plea that constitutional processes were being followed.

However, the appointment of the CAG in 2013 brought this issue to the fore again. The appointment of the CAG was challenged in the Supreme Court with the petitioner contending that that there was serious conflict of interest as the appointee had served as the director-general of acquisitions in the Ministry of Defence from 2003 to 2010 and subsequently as defence secretary. The deals during his period of office in the ministry are being investigated for kickback allegations. The petitioner further contended that the appointee was given a year's extension to ensure that he takes over as CAG after the current incumbent retires. The Supreme Court rejected the plea, seeking quashing of the appointment on the consideration that it was the prerogative of the government to appoint a CAG (*Business Standard* 22 May 2013).[1]

WEAKNESS IN IMPACT

Mode of appointment apart, there are some limitations to the functioning of CAG. There is considerable delay in the submission of appropriation of accounts. Neither does the CAG have the power to question the officers who have committed irregularities nor does he have the power to hold the persons responsible for the loss caused to exchequer. This is, of course, combined with delays in presenting audit reports and reluctance of the government in responding to its objections. However, in placing its reports in the public domain, the CAG has strengthened the citizen's ability to know how the government functions. Unless information is available, accountability mechanisms cannot function well.

It is this process that is weak for many reasons despite establishing the principle of accountability. The parliamentary committee is unable to deliberate on audit objections unless the government agencies respond to them. This means that the accountability

[1] Names for the appointment for the position of CAG emerge through usual government processes and are sent to the prime minister for approval. The professional experience reflects the rotating nature of jobs that an IAS officer goes through in his career. The last appointment held also shows no particular pattern with the last three having held the positions of defence secretary, secretary, financial services, and petroleum secretary.

framework also provides for not only response of the government but also an account of the remedial measures undertaken. There is no mechanism that can either enforce a response or make it available on time. The result is that in a large number of cases, audit remarks and objections are not responded to by governments. It becomes difficult to know if any remedial measures are undertaken.

There is another issue involved. Audit reports usually document deviations that took place several years ago, possibly during the time when either officials involved in irregular practices have changed or the government has taken remedial measures. Das (2005:136) has drawn attention to the comment of the Fifth Pay Commission which said:

> Audit should be as concurrent as possible. Scandals and scams are known even while they are being planned and executed. If audit draws attention to them forthwith in well publicized manner, such scandals can be halted in mid-stride. Post-mortems are useful but can only be conducted while the patient is dead. It is better to cure the patient and try to keep him alive.

In some cases, however, the CAG has come out with concurrent audit reports that have had significant political bearing. Earlier, it happened at the time of Rajiv Gandhi in the case of buying defence equipment, and recently in 2010–13 in case of selling licenses for operating coal fields and telecom spectrum. All these cases pointed to high political functionaries who were the decision-makers and were alleged not to have followed dues process, which resulted in heavy loss to the government. This raised quite a public uproar, leading to tarring of the government of corruption and resignation of ministers.

The impact of the functioning of the CAG on making the government agencies accountable has been marginal. This has happened in spite of the constitutional mandate of the institution, its statutory independence from the executive, its diligence, and so on (Das 2005). Part of the responsibility for this ineffective accountability framework has to be shouldered by Parliament. As already mentioned, it finds little time for such matters and members do not take up the issues raised in audit reports for critically appraising the government.

With all its weaknesses, the CAG has been a significant constitutional position holding the government accountable for its financial management. The audit reports have raised political controversies, which have served the purpose of highlighting issues of maladministration in public domain.

THE CAG AND PPPs

In recent times, particularly after the investment strategy laid down in 11th and 12th Five-Year Plans, increasing investment is taking place in the PPP mode, but efforts are being made to limit the mandate of CAG in auditing these institutions. The CAG issued guidelines for auditing infrastructure projects in the PPP mode in 2009. These guidelines stressed that the basic objective of audit of PPP projects is 'to provide unbiased, objective assessment of whether public resources are responsibly and effectively managed to achieve intended results, namely to verify value-for-money aspects'. The guidelines point out that PPP arrangements attempt to marry the conflicting approaches of the two partners in the arrangement, namely the responsibility of the public sector to provide services at a reasonable cost to the public and the motive of the private sector to maximize profits.

However, audit reports have not yet been commissioned on this basis. It appears that the government has not given an audit mandate to the CAG, which is a normal requirement. While it is true that the CAG issued audit guidelines in 2009, speaking at the National Academy of Audit and Accounts in 2011, the CAG is reported to have said that the audit mandate should be expanded to bring all public expenditure including PPPs in its purview. He further added that there is a strong need for an efficient system of audit for successful delivery of government services. The public demand for transparency in government programmes, including PPP projects, is likely to increase manifold in the days to come (Nidhi Sharma 2011). There is a simultaneous resistance to allow CAG scrutiny of PPPs. The Planning Commission opposed the proposal to bring PPP projects under CAG scrutiny and stated that the CAG should not have jurisdiction over projects that have private sector involvement. As stated by the Planning Commission's deputy chairman, 'The performance of the public part of the [PPP] project should be subjected to proper scrutiny but obviously where the private sector [is given] flexibility... . You cannot subject that to CAG scrutiny' (*Deccan Herald* 13 September 2011).

The rising dissatisfaction and lack of clarity in the role of the CAG has given rise to the demand in Public Accounts Committee that it should go beyond the reports of the CAG and have the capacity to take up scrutiny of projects on its own while seeking the help of CAG (*The Hindu Business* line, 5 June 2012). It has also been reported in the same write-up that a bill seeking to expand the scope of the CAG to scrutinize PPP projects besides regulators including SEBI, TRAI, and IRDA is under the consideration of the Finance Ministry. The bill seeks to replace the CAG Act of 1971.

Despite all the hesitation of government in allowing CAG to audit PPP projects, the CAG has submitted an audit report on the partnership with GMR that constructed the Indira Gandhi International airport. The report examined government decisions taken in the implementation of the partnership and pointed out: 'Whenever DIAL [the private partner] has raised an issue regarding revenue to it or expenditure to be debited to government in contravention to the provisions of OMDA [Operation, Maintenance and Development Agreement], the ministry and the Airports Authority of India have always ruled in favour of the operators and against the interest of the government.' Then the report cites specific instances to substantiate this comment (see *Indian Express* 24 May 2012). The

CAG again made an effort to audit the PPP projects in airports in Delhi and Mumbai. It was reported (*Hindustan Times* 21 October 2015) that the government will view the failure to furnish financial records for scrutiny by the government or its nominee (read CAG) as a breach of the agreement. But the same report ended by quoting an official of the two PPP operating units as saying, 'Projects developed under public–private partnerships programme do not come under the purview of the CAG.'

The Supreme Court, on the other hand, throwing out the petitions of telecom operators in 2014, had established the principle that the CAG was empowered to examine the accounts of the private telecom operators that share revenue with the government on spectrum use. The court justifies its stand by emphasizing that CAG's examination of accounts of service providers in a revenue-sharing contract is extremely important to ascertain whether there is unlawful gain to the service provider and an unlawful loss to the Union because the revenue generated out of the partnership has to be credited to the Consolidated Fund. A recent judgment of the Delhi High Court has upheld the principle that the CAG was empowered to examine the accounts of private telecom operators that share revenue with government on spectrum use (see *Hindustan Times* 31 October 2015).

The CAG in its report no. 2 (2014: para 7.3) reiterated that a private player cannot be outside parliamentary oversight as he delivers public services for which he gets paid from public funds or by users (citizens) through payment of user fee/tariff. Citing section 20 (1) of CAG Act 1971, the CAG recommended that appropriate clauses in the PPP agreement may be considered by the government to ensure that all PPP agreements with private bodies contain provisions for parliamentary oversight by subjecting the accounts of the PPPs to comprehensive audit by CAG.

Kelkar Committee reporting towards the end of 2015 agreed with concerns expressed by both the government and private parties against the demand for audit of PPP projects and revealing information through the Right to Information (RTI) Act. The committee contended that 'conventional audit by authority of private parties' books per standard procurement procedures risks delivery of poor quality of service and public assets' and recommended that the statutory bodies be clearly defined through overarching mechanism.

Clamour for the need for formal audit of these PPP projects and their parliamentary scrutiny rises as more and more comments about their wasteful expenditures, rising costs, and transferring their cost burden to the government or citizens multiply. In the construction of international airports at Bengaluru, Hyderabad, and Delhi, these inadequacies are made pointedly.

PARLIAMENTARY ROLE

Parliament has also failed to demand more accountability through its debates or question hour. This method, however, has been inadequate possibly because of the dispersed nature of information and, of course, lack of interest. Little information has been revealed through the question mode; questions have really provided an opportunity to the government to continue to emphasize the strategy of using PPPs to implement projects and assure Parliament of its success (Mathur et al. 2013: 25–8).

What is striking is that as the government goes on to create special purpose institutions through PPPs, there is little effort to evaluate their performance or hold them accountable. Every effort is being made by the government to keep them out of the purview of traditional accountability mechanisms or those created recently through the RTI Act of 2005. A uniform policy of arriving at PPP mode of implementing programmes is being chosen in physical infrastructure as well as social sectors without recognizing the difference in character and purpose of the project.

Civil society organizations have been quite active in demanding transparency in agreements signed between public and private partners, and the Resident Welfare Association was able to make an inroad into the shroud of confidentiality of National Highways Authority of India (NHAI). Ahuja (2010) reports in *Hindustan Times* that Dwarka residents have won a year-long battle against the NHAI and made it agree to upload the agreement it entered into with Japanese DSC for the construction and operation of Gurgaon expressway on its website. Costing about ₹1,000 crores, the agreement was signed in 2002.

In a significant episode that reflects on the way officials of the NHAI responded to civil society organizations that had to launch agitations and demonstrations for accountability, the CAG report also received flak from the public. The NHAI hit back at the CAG for his report on the NHAI's recent performance in the highway projects on PPP mode, highlighting major mismanagement and irregularities. Stating the central auditor 'lacks understanding of the whole concept of PPP', the chairman of the NHAI said that they were ready to discuss all issues raised by CAG at a public forum where business organizations would also be invited (Dash 2014).

ACCOUNTABILITY OF PPPs

In discussing the pursuit of PPPs as an alternative strategy to promote development programmes and implement them, we had suggested that investments in such a strategy continue unabated despite the lack of evidence that they are effective in delivering public goods and services. There is little evaluation of these projects and 'there is nothing to inform the concerned citizen about their impact except what the organizations themselves choose to report' (Ravindran 2011: 52).

The fact that there is lack of accountability of these institutions and they are being established without evaluating their experience needs to be underlined. Notably, in India the changes in governance structures and adoption of PPP projects are taking place in the absence of any specific law or regulatory authority governing concession contracts that details guidelines for adequate service, the users' rights and liabilities, the tariff policy, the bidding process, requirements of a concession contract, the duties of the granting authority and concessionaire, appropriate conditions for intervention and termination of the concessions, and transparency. While there is no study to highlight these in India, where PPP is still at a nascent stage, studies in other countries do suggest that issues of accountability often have been compromised in the implementation of PPP projects. For instance, Alison Mohr, in her study of London and Copenhagen underground projects under PPP, points out:

> Principles such as transparency and fairness often associated with the state, have been brought into question by the creation of institutional linkages with private sector organizations within which the delivery of public services is now being managed. Indeed, there is growing evidence that the contractual relations of public private partnerships have led to a clear weakening of traditional notions of accountability reflecting both a shift to new lines of accountability (private sector shareholders) and vicious circle of monitoring and distrust between partner organizations. (Mohr 2004)

Moreover, changing structures and complex contractual relations require information in the public domain, in order to protect the rights of the citizens. This, however, has been lacking with many of the PPP projects that have been implemented.

The PPPs with definitional ambiguities, a neoliberal agenda, and managerial thrust in governance demand a more concerted exploration of their functioning in a democratic setting. Questions of accountability become complex as PPPs are introduced in infrastructural sector and in social sectors. This diversity raises different kinds of issues as the purposes of different PPPs may vary. Does the question of accountability have the same salience across all sectors? This is an important question to ask because promoting private investment in social sectors is quite different from that in the sector of physical infrastructure.

12 Social Mobilization for Public Accountability

A pillar of democratic accountability is the availability of adequate information in the public domain about the functioning of the government. India had an Official Secrets Act passed during the colonial times that was not repealed after Independence and continued to function as a barrier to those who sought information from the government about its decisions and the processes of taking those decisions. It has taken a long people's struggle to make the government enact the RTI legislation in 2005. There had been sporadic rulings of the Supreme Court which in 1975 said:

> In a government of responsibility like ours, where the agents of the public must be responsible there can be but few secrets. The people of this country have a right to know every public act, everything that is done in a public way by their functionaries. They are entitled to know the particulars of every public transaction in all its bearings.[1]

In a subsequent judgment in 1982, the Supreme Court followed this up by ruling that 'the concept of an open government is the direct emanation from the right to know, which seems implicit in the right to free speech and expression guaranteed under Article

---

[1] *State of UP* vs *Raj Narain 1975*, quoted in RAAG and CES Report (2014:17).

19(1)a',[2] thus characterizing it as a fundamental right. However, despite these rulings and some environmental disasters such as the Bhopal gas tragedy, it was a people's movement that led the government to enact the legislation such as the RTI Act in 2005.

The enactment of RTI Act in India in 2005 has been hailed as radical, if not a revolutionary, policy change. It has been a significant departure from the established administrative practices that had a long past. After the USA passed its Freedom of Information Act in 1966, India was among the many countries that followed suit. Initially, this movement for transparency in government was confined to some countries in the Western world, but it gained momentum in the Third World countries after 1990. In the 220 years from 1766, when the first transparency law was passed in Sweden, till 1995, less than 20 countries had such laws (Singh 2011). More than 90 countries around the world have now adopted Freedom of Information Acts of varying scope and degree of effectiveness to facilitate access to records held by government bodies and another 50 have pending efforts.

The RTI Act 2005, as mentioned in the beginning of the chapter, has been hailed as radical, if not a revolutionary, policy change. The reason is that the government had been working with a colonial Official Secrets Act 1923, justifying withholding any information from the citizens as it found appropriate in a particular case. The government withheld information regarding several incidents such as the Bhopal gas tragedy, or the people's resistance to deforestation in the Himalayas, or to the construction of the Sardar Sarovar Dam, which triggered initial protests about the use of this Act. Demands from civil society organizations to scrap the Act grew. The government made several statements to the effect that major changes are going to be brought about in the Official Secrets Act but it

---

[2] *State of UP* vs *Raj Narain 1975*, quoted in RAAG and CES Report (2014:17).

remained to be seen whether this was going to happen and to what extent. There have been, in the past, several attempts to amend the Official Secrets Act, but in the absence of genuine political and administrative will, and popular pressure, all these initiatives came to naught. A working group was formed by the Government of India in 1977 to look into required amendments to the Official Secrets Act to enable greater dissemination of information to the public. This group recommended that no change was required in the Act as it pertained only to protect national safety and not to prevent legitimate release of information to the public. In 1989, yet another committee was set up, which recommended restriction of the areas where governmental information could be hidden, and recommended opening up of all other spheres of information. However, no legislation followed these recommendations (Mander and Joshi 1999).[3] The Official Secrets Act created a culture of secrecy within administration and soon developed political overtones.

RISE OF THE SOCIAL MOVEMENT

The demand for the passage of the RTI Act is seen to rise from the efforts of social and people's movements. These seem to have begun sometime in the 1980s. Singh (2011:54–5) points out that there were three kinds of stakeholders. One, there were people's movements working on ensuring basic economic rights and access to government schemes for the rural poor. The relevance and importance of transparency was brought home to them when they found that the landless workers in rural areas were often cheated and not paid their full wages. Yet the workers could not challenge the paymasters, who claimed that they had worked for fewer days

---

[3] There was an earlier attempt to examine this Act by the First Administrative Reforms Commission set up in 1966 but the recommendations of its study team were not included in the final report of the commission (see Sharma 2013:177 and Srivastava 2009:114).

than they actually had, as these workers were denied access to the attendance register in which they affixed their thumb impression every day they worked, because these were government records. Second, the group that joined this movement was that of those fighting for the human rights of various groups and individuals in conflict-prone areas of India. The third group of supporters were environmentalists who were concerned about the rapid destruction and degradation of the environment. They were spurred by the success, though limited, of an earlier petition to the Supreme Court demanding transparency about the environment.[4]

These civil society activists were joined by urban activists consisting of various hues of intellectuals and civil servants. But the role of the peoples' protests that were leading to a mass disaffection towards secrecy due to suppressive measures of the government was the core of the movement. What provided greater momentum to the RTI movement was the beginning of a rural movement around 1990 started by Mazdoor Kisan Shakti Sangathan (MKSS) in Rajasthan, demanding access to information on behalf of wage workers and small farmers who were denied benefit of their rightful wages or their just benefits under government schemes. Singh (2011: 55) suggests that MKSS transformed the RTI movement, which metamorphosed into a mass movement. As documented in Roy and others (2001), the people began to understand that their livelihood, wages, and employment depended a great deal on the investments made by the government as a development agency. If these benefits were not accruing, then they had a right to know where the investment occurred and how much was actually spent and what was given out as wages. The right to economic well-being got translated into right to information.

---

[4] The environmental movement has been the precursor of the struggle for transparency, and some of those who were active in it also joined the present movement for RTI.

The *jan sunwai*s (public hearings) are mentioned as the core strategy that moved the Rajasthan government and caught the imagination of the people. As Roy and others point out, the struggle became for '*hamara paisa hamara hamara hisaab*' (our money, our account), which became a critical issue in these public hearings. The essence of the campaign that steamrolled into a movement was the jan sunwais where villagers assembled to testify whether the public works that had been met out of the expenditures certified by the government actually exist. If they did, then were the wages disbursed as stipulated? The movement gathered steam 1996 onwards, and ultimately the chief minister of Rajasthan announced that the people had the right to demand and receive details of expenditure on development works in the villages.

As the demand for transparency spread, it was felt that a national body for coordinating efforts for the formulation of a national legislation be formed. A group of urban activists based in Delhi consisting of eminent journalists, lawyers, and academics, joined hands, and after a series of consultations, the National Campaign for People's Right to Information (NCPRI) was born and located in Delhi. It consisted of a few rural activists and their voice was that of Aruna Roy, who led the MKSS movement in Rajasthan.

This group entrusted Justice P.B. Sawant to frame a model RTI bill. Members of the group carried on a campaign to bring the issue on public agenda through meetings, conferences, and media. The Government of India came under public pressure and as a first step appointed a working group on Right to Information and Promotion of Open and Transparent Government in 1997.

The working group placed its tasks within the broad framework of democracy and accountability and emphasized that 'democracy means choice and a sound and informed choice is possible only on the possible of information' (Government of India 1997: 3). It accepted following broad principles in the formulation of legislation: (*i*) disclosure of information should be the rule and secrecy the exception (*ii*) the exceptions should be clearly defined, and (*iii*) there should be an independent mechanism for adjudication of disputes between the citizens and public authorities.

It took another five years before the then government enacted the Freedom of Information Act in 2002. What is significant is that the Supreme Court had established that access to information was a right, as guaranteed under the Constitution. It was not merely a largesse that a benevolent government provided to its citizens. Thus, the fight for this right was a struggle for democracy and not for mere good governance. It is important to keep this point in mind for there is a distinction between the nomenclature of the Act passed by the NDA government in 2002 and the one passed by UPA government in 2005. One is titled Freedom of Information and the other Right to Information. This changed the nature of the struggle after 2005 when the government began implementing it while the 2002 Act never got off the statute book.

Possible reason why the nomenclature 'freedom' was used during the NDA regime could be twofold: it was a product of bureaucratic thinking and lacked people's participation. And, it has been reported, that the NDA government had sent a team of officers abroad to learn from the experience of other countries which were possibly using the nomenclature freedom rather than right. This change was also embedded in the larger vocabulary of the civil society movements. With increased awareness and civil society activism, the political discourse was changing and many of the struggles being spearheaded by the civil society organizations were demanding citizens' rights, whether they were in the field of food, work, or education (see Chandhoke 2007).

In 2004, the government changed and the UPA government led by the Congress party came into power. The Congress party had already put right to information on its election manifesto and appeared favourable to the passage of the Act. After Sonia Gandhi, as leader of the party, rejected the position of prime minister, she formed the National Advisory Council (NAC), which consisted of members from civil society organizations, civil servants who had become social activists, and also Aruna Roy, who led the MKSS and who was also a member of the core group of NCPRI. This council was to push for many welfare measures in the rural sector. As an undisputed leader of the Congress party and having the responsibility of implementing the provisions in the party's manifesto, she commanded a lot of influence with the government.

On 16 August 2004, Sonia Gandhi, as the chairperson of the NAC, dispatched a letter on the RTI to the government urging it to introduce an amended Freedom of Information Act in Parliament at the earliest. All the background material needed for this letter had been prepared by NCPRI. The momentum began to build up. Not only were recommendations being made to the government by the NAC, but separate communications were also being initiated by the chairperson of the NAC to the prime minister. In 2005, RTI was enacted after considerable lobbying with bureaucratic and political leadership.

It is clear from above-mentioned arguments that the passage of this Act was possible only when the active support of the political as well as bureaucratic elite was available.

Very soon after the enactment of the Act, however, the government's reluctance to open itself for public scrutiny began to manifest itself in the efforts at amending the Act and limiting its scope. All the six main political parties had rejected the plea of the Act that they too be brought under its purview. This emboldened the Ministry of Personnel to propose amendments to the Act in 2010. Even though this effort was not successful at that time, Prime Minister Manmohan Singh expressed his misgivings about the scope of the Act too.

The process followed in seeking information from the government is that a citizen applies to the relevant department, which should be provided within 30 days. If the reply is unsatisfactory or delayed, the citizen can appeal to central information commissioner (CIC) for redress. One effective bureaucratic way to stall giving information is to allow for appeals to CIC. This process can take time. Appeals can lead to long correspondence between the CIC and the relevant government department or the appeal may not be taken up due to inability to handle the accumulating number of appeals. The result is that administration can effectively block the intended results of the Act. As of June 2015, around 35,000 to 40,000 cases were pending on appeal before the Information Commission.

Another strategy can be delaying the appointment of information commissioners. It takes a long time before a CIC gets appointed and sometimes the process gets delayed for a year or more. In another characteristic, mostly retired civil servants have been appointed as CICs. The eligibility conditions for the appointment mentions that they must be 'persons of eminence in public life with wide knowledge and experience in law science and technology, social service, management, journalism, mass media or administration and governance'. The government has mostly found retired civil servants, usually from the IAS/IPS, in this category. It has yet to be assessed whether public knowledge of the way the government functions has helped in changing it. Many officials schooled in the earlier tradition are reluctant to part with information and this makes the task of implementing the Act more onerous. This may be one reason why the government seems to rely on retired civil servants and also a reason why a large number of appeals pile up and the commission is unable to dispose them off in timely fashion.[5]

---

[5] A recent report (*Times of India* 13 April 2018) points out that the activists feel that this effort to devalue the position of information commissioners continues. The government is considering downgrading the status of the CIC in terms of salary and allowances from being equivalent to that of a Supreme Court judge to a secretary in the Government of India.

What is clear from the aforementioned arguments is that the government's response to instruments of accountability is not very favourable. The Parliament has not been alert and does not signal its seriousness in holding the administration accountable in its day-to-day actions. It is this broad political environment that sets the stage for holding PPPs accountable.

RTI AND PPPs

First, let us look at the issue of information gathering before referring to accountability mechanism. PPPs can be held accountable only if reliable information about their conduct is available in the public domain. Transparency, therefore, is the key to creating accountability (Streets 2004:12). Access to information has been seen as a critical measure for an effective accountability mechanism and it has been pointed out that a major step towards holding government networks as accountable as possible is to make their activity as visible as possible to legislators, interest groups, and ordinary citizens by ensuring that they operate in a real or virtual public space (Slaughter 2004:172).

Recognizing this significance of transparency in creating effective accountability, the enactment of RTI Act 2005 has to be welcomed. But in its implementation, PPPs have suffered a fate similar to one they suffered under public audit, and this is what we turn to. PPP has been seen as the way forward in order to deliver services to the public. However, the scrutiny of such projects which are in the public domain and serve the general public has been marred with hurdles. Even the RTI Act, which is seen as one of the most

> empowering laws enacted in independent India, which has brought power in the hands of the 'little man', has not been able to make PPP transparent to the common man. While there is no doubt that the governments, both at the Centre and the states, are obliged to provide information sought by any person under the Act, the Indian

courts are yet to decide whether PPP projects are to be treated as commercial ventures and retained outside the purview of the Act or subjected to the same levels of accountability as expected from a democratically elected government and its various organs. (Sharma 2010)

In spite of this Act, civil society organizations have had to make appeals to the Central Information Commission to get information released from PPPs. The bone of contention is whether such projects come under the ambit of being a 'public authority' or not. The argument which is given in favour of bringing PPP projects under the RTI scanner is that any project which 'involves the government in any capacity should be subject to the same checks and balances as the government itself' and 'any kind of opaqueness could make it a platform for looting resources through the unholy political–business–bureaucracy nexus' (Sebastian 2011). The counter argument is that 'business and governance must never be mixed'. One of the main arguments given in favour of bringing PPP under RTI is that 'private players under the RTI purview come under the definition of "public authority" as per Section 2(h) of the Act'. Here, this includes 'non-government organization substantially financed, directly or indirectly by funds' provided by the government. 'Whenever a government gives something, it is a partnership. It could be in the form of public funding or giving of monopoly or land or rights', says Information Commissioner Shailesh Gandhi. The various concessions and the viability gap funding that a PPP gets can amount to substantial financing, says Venkatesh Nayak of Commonwealth Human Rights Initiative.

There has also been a tug of war between the Planning Commission and the CIC on bringing PPP projects under RTI.

In July 2011 the Chief Information Commissioner Satyananda Mishra wrote to the Planning Commission deputy Chairman Montek Singh Ahluwalia to incorporate disclosure norms, so that any project which has the participation of private firms and

concessioners come under the purview of the transparency legislation. The decision came about after a full commission meeting on
December 28, wherein all information commissioners agreed that a
specific disclosure clause should be included in the model concessionaire agreement (MCA) between the government and the private party. (Sharma 2011)

The CIC is further reported to have written that once such
conditions are built into the PPP agreements and the private parties
willingly subject themselves to such conditions, a lot of confusion
in this regards will cease to exist and citizens will have access to
vital information regarding projects which affect their lives. The
CIC had also suggested that the PPP agreement should include a
necessary condition that the special purpose vehicle or any other
entity which comes into being as a result of the PPP would be a
public authority within the meaning of section 2(h) of the RTI Act
(Chauhan 2011).

However, the Planning Commission in March 2011 rejected the
proposal of the CIC with Montek Singh Ahluwalia stating that the
'RTI is not Right to Information on private companies. It per-
tains to information on public authority' (*Indian Express* 2011). The
deputy chairman of the Planning Commission is reported to have
questioned how a concessionaire, a private firm performs its job is
not a relevant issue from the point of view of RTI. As a response to
the CIC's proposal, the Planning Commission sought the advice of
the Ministry of Law and Justice. The response of the ministry came
in July 2011. It overruled the application of RTI to PPP projects,
saying that law does not allow private executioners of the projects
to be declared public authorities. Shailesh Gandhi termed the ver-
dict as being a 'violation of the transparency law and felt that it was
now up to the civil society to take up the issue' (Gandhi 2015).
But once again in October 2011, Montek Singh Ahluwalia was
in favour of scrutinizing PPP projects via RTI; however, he stated
that 'PPP should be covered under the RTI Act, but government

agency should reply to the information sought' (*Times of India* 2011). It should not be applicable to private companies, as only public authorities are covered under the law. This duality which does not focus its attention on a PPP project is yet to be resolved.

Let us point out in conclusion that the first step towards accountability is transparency. Full information about the project, its financial outlays, and functions and obligations should be in the public domain. One goes forward towards redressal of grievance or holding the project and its functionaries accountable when this information is available. But as we have narrated, there has been great reluctance in allowing this to happen in India. This is in spite of the RTI Act and the Central Information Commission coming out in support of demands for information. Notably, the Planning Commission is against bringing such projects under the ambit of the RTI Act, with the Deputy Chairperson Montek Singh Ahluwalia once again stating that though PPP should be covered under the RTI Act, there should be *flexibility* for the private players, and only the government agency should reply to the information sought—exempting public accountability of private players and the real accountability of 'partnerships'.

STRUGGLE FOR LOKPAL

While the passage of the RTI Act was seen as an achievement of civil society action, there was disappointment that it did not lead to the government becoming more transparent. There was reluctance to put more information in the public domain and the government responded only when it was sought by a citizen. Decision-making processes still remained opaque. This disappointment was reflected in increasing concerns about spreading big ticket corruption in the country.

The impetus from the passage of the RTI Act led many civil society organizations to turn their attention to demanding the revival of the proposal to appoint a *lokpal* (ombudsman). India against Corruption, led by Anna Hazare, is one of the largest organization working towards this cause. His team consisted of former police officers, professional lawyers, social activists, and others. Prominent among them were Prashant Bhushan, an activist-lawyer, and Arvind Kejriwal, a Magsaysay award winner, a graduate of IIT, and former civil servant. Others who joined in were Baba Ramdev, spiritual guru and a popular yoga teacher with a very large following.

The movement gained momentum when Hazare undertook a fast unto death on 5 April 2011. A frail looking person reflecting a Gandhian image with no ambition for power fired the imagination of the people. He had earlier acquired fame for his constructive work in a village in Maharashtra. At one point it was reported that more than a lakh people gathered at the place where he was undertaking his fast in Delhi. Hazare and his associates were seen as renunciates rather than people bidding for a role for themselves in the power structure. This perhaps got thousands of young people and professionals out on to public places to hold a candle and rail against corruption (Ananth 2011: 21).

What brought a spurt to the movement was the support that it got from media. Mohapatra (2013) has argued that media transformed an agitation into a movement and the protests were termed as 'second freedom movement', 'august *kranti*', and so on. Urban middle class took to Facebook and Twitter to protest. Political parties did not come out in support and it was reported that when one or two politicians wanted to join the rally, they were turned away by the organizers.

LOKPAL BILL

The basic idea of having a lokpal was mooted in 1968, and a bill was introduced 1969. It did not go through the Rajya Sabha. Subsequent versions of the bill were introduced several times, but none of them reached any stage of deliberation. The demand of the Hazare movement was to frame a law that gave enforcement power to the office and was autonomous of the government. A further demand was that a joint committee including members from the civil society and the government should be formed to frame the legislation. Amidst the chorus from Parliamentarians that only Parliament can frame a law, a ten-member drafting committee was formed with equal representation of both the sides. This happened after four days of fasting.

From the very beginning, there were fundamental differences between the two sides over the officials to be covered including the prime minister, enforcing agencies, processes of appointment, extent of autonomy, and so on. These were hotly contentious issues and the talks broke down. Hazare had given up his fast but threatened to undertake it again. He followed his threat and began his fast a couple of months later. This fast lasted 12 days and resulted in Parliament unanimously passing a 'Sense of the House' resolution accepting some of the principles set out by the Hazare team.

In the winter session of Parliament, the Lokpal Bill was introduced but the Hazare team expressed dissatisfaction with many of its provisions. However, the bill was passed in the Lok Sabha but could not muster support in the Rajya Sabha. It was ultimately passed in 2013 after a consideration of the Select Committee and received assent of the president in 2014.

The Act as passed does not fully satisfy the civil society campaigning for it, but some of them do accept that if properly implemented, it should provide a significant deterrent to corruption, especially the high-level corruption that seems to have become increasingly common in India. They further suggest that this can happen if adequate human and financial resources are provided and there is political will among the top political and bureaucratic leadership to make this institution succeed (Johri et al. 2014).

The appointment of Lokpal is still in a limbo.[6] Rules have not been framed and resources have not been provided for its establishment. Thus, what is happening is that the legacy of keeping information on administrative decision-making out of bounds of citizens is still ruling the mindset of the government. While it is largely accepted that certain strategic and critical areas demand certain amount of secrecy, this principle does not hold for all administrative activity. But as emphasized by Gandhi (2015:150–1), in writing about the performance of RTI, Indian citizens are increasingly using it to empower themselves. More and more information is coming out in the public domain and has the potential of transforming the way administration functions. However, as privatization occurs and PPPs go out of the domain of RTI, the transformation may be limited and such a hope may be belied.

[6] In response to a PIL filed in April 2017, the Supreme Court directed the government to appoint Lokpal as there is no justification to hold it back till the proposed amendment to include the leader of the single largest opposition party instead of the leader of the opposition is passed. However, the leader of the main opposition party has refused to join the Selection Committee as he is being included as a special invitee and not as a member (see *Indian Express* 11 April 2018).

13 Reform or Silent Revolution

Successive governments in India have publicly remonstrated against the public administration they inherited at the time of Independence from British colonial rule. A large number of committees and commissions were established to suggest reforms and changes that would reflect the new concerns of these governments. International experts, particularly from the USA, were also invited to make their recommendations and lend prestige and legitimacy to this endeavour. As we have shown, little substantive change happened on the ground. Reports were archived as the commissions and committees wound up their work and as the international experts left the Indian shores. Enthusiasm for reform withers away and the pursuit of reform becomes a symbolic act.

However, the advent of neoliberalism as an overarching framework for state activities induced introduction of administrative institutions that would have a far-reaching impact on the way state implements public policies. These institutions are being established to deliver public goods and services in a way that keeps the formal conventional institutions in place but erodes away their full responsibility of doing so. These new institutions mark the acceptance of the idea that private business sector and civil society organizations can deliver public goods and services without affecting the prime goal of state to serve public interest. And that they can do it more efficiently and effectively is the most attractive part of this idea.

Apparently, a distinctive goal of state renovation is being pursued, but as the change in conventional public administration is not yielding results, a parallel system in being constructed. There is an urgency to this construction because it is believed that this will promote development, which is seen as increased participation in the world of global and liberalized economy. It is this perspective that provides a framework of what has come to be known as 'governance reforms' in which the public sector is designed to do less and less and make an orderly retreat to have limited assignments.

A significant aspect of these governance reforms in India is that new institutions under its rubric are being established as an addition to the already established administrative institutional framework, and the expectation is that the two will go happily together. A kind of layering is taking place—old structures do not die as the new come up. Most sectors are now afflicted with this perspective. Build smart cities but allow the existing ones to languish. Let the public health system struggle but privatize health services and so on. This story repeats itself in education and even in physical infrastructure sectors. The assertion that public administration is becoming increasingly complex does not adequately reflect the picture that is emerging. It is becoming complicated, and complicated public administration probably demands a new definition of public administration itself.

However, this way of introducing greater capacity to deliver public services betrays little understanding of what administrative reform is all about. Liberal perspective has encouraged governments to reduce the scope of state activities. Public administration is shedding its many activities as the scope of the state gets narrowed. The slogan of governance reforms is 'less of government, more of governance'. But reducing the scope of administrative activities is not the same as administrative reform. Earlier narratives of the first 30 years of the Plan period were focused on strengthening the capacity of the administrative system to deliver public goods. Structural change, procedural change, and attitudinal change were the terms that emerged from most reports of committees and commissions established to suggest reforms. Reforms were seen necessary to serve the poor and the outliers in society. Critics highlighted these issues in public discourse.

The buzzwords of the liberal era are privatization, PPPs, and semi-autonomous institutions free from political control. The goal is of achieving efficiency in delivering public services. Reducing the role of the public sector and increasing that of the private sector is seen as reform for it is assumed that it alone can provide efficiency in delivering public services. Strengthening public administration as such through reform is not seen as a worthwhile pursuit anymore.

What is happening is that the government's perception of reform has been diverted from strengthening state capacity to limiting the scope of state activities. These are two distinct perspectives. Fukuyama (2004) urges that this distinction needs to be recognized and argues that the 'strength of state institutions is more important in a broad sense than the scope of state functions' (Fukuyama 2004: 25). Liberalization focused on expanding the role of the private sector and limiting the scope of public sector. This focus neglected the thrust towards administrative reform. However, the importance of reforming traditional administration came back again on the public agenda as liberalization proceeded when the Second Administrative Reforms Commission was appointed in 2006. It submitted its last report in 2009, which was then soon forgotten. The new government that was installed in 2014 has not yet shown any inkling of the way it goes about reform, though it continues to stress its commitment to limit the scope of state activities.

Why is it that administrative reform has been so difficult and trimming the scope of public administration comparatively much easier? First reason, of course, is the acceptance of a liberal ideology and relating development to a globalized world. Markets have ascended to a primary role, while state has been constrained in its activities. It is now generally agreed that the significant role of the public sector is to have less of it and the critical tactical question is how to make this retreat orderly (Roberts 2010: 4). This ready acceptance of liberal ideology has stemmed from dissatisfaction with the performance of traditional public administration in delivering public services. But this may be true only for the era beginning in 1991 when the economy was opened up and the private sector was accorded a more important role in development. This ideological turn led to governance reforms that could facilitate the emergence of the private sector. Focus on public administration declined in the process.

If this is an explanation for the neglect of administrative reform in the era of liberalization and globalization, what happened when the state was the major actor in development, liberalization was not on the horizon, and the government was concerned that its development policies will not be implemented adequately by the administration in the country inherited from colonial rule? Our earlier argument was that the governing elite found that it was possible to work with the system and all that was needed was to bend it or tweak it for the purposes required. The reports on the functioning of administration during the period of Emergency, 1975–7, testify to the ways that this could be done. Later years sought loyalty of administrators to work the system, and a transfer industry spawned to create an incentive system. Rent-seeking administrative positions were seen as reward for loyalty and the administrative system moulded itself to reflect the requirements of the post-Independence governing elite.

However, this formulation appears to be an outcome of a deeper process at work. This is concerned with the way democracy has functioned, and Miller and Fox (2007) have called it a 'loop model'. It is assumed that the people are sovereign because they vote and authorize a government to act on their behalf. The government represents them and it is expected that it will take their concerns into account while framing policies. Representation also serves a parallel function of accountability and a promise of faith to the democratic sovereign. Miller and Fox (2007) further argue that this model is mythical because people's concerns and demands can be manipulated and candidates are seldom elected on specific policy issues or rational considerations.

What this means is that democratically elected governments do not necessarily reflect the needs of the people they represent. There is now a vast literature in the social sciences that depicts the formation of elite groups after elections that determine policies that serve their interests. These elite groups consist of interests of bureaucracy, politicians, military or big business, and organized labour. These are the players in the policy process who petition the government not only about grievances, but also for largesse. Terms such as military–industrial complex, iron triangles, policy community, and so on capture the closed nature of everyday policy making, directing the eye toward particularistic and narrow perspectives that cannot credibly be said to be fundamentally concerned with the public interest (Miller and Fox 2007: 5–6).

This approach has much to tell us about the lack of policy concern for administrative reform in India. While public policies during the Plan period had the basic refrain of removing poverty and helping the common man, they served the interests of the elite in their implementation. In a widely read and quoted analysis, Bardhan (1984) showed how certain groups consisting of industrial business class, rich farmers, and professionals (both civil and military), including white collar workers, influenced public policies and twisted them to benefit themselves, leaving little investment for pursuing pro-public interest goals. While there were conflicts among them, they were usually resolved to serve their broad interests. Primary education was neglected and so was primary health care. Much was made of village upliftment, but little serious action followed. If corruption was an issue, it stemmed from the way rural programmes were implemented, and the administration cared little if the money for the poor did not reach them. Administration thus became an instrument of the elite.

Industrialization of the economy was the major concern and the lead role was given to the state. A vast regulatory mechanism was established to monitor the activities of private business houses and direct them towards the goals of the state. In designing these new agencies, the principles of existing administrative practice were accepted. It then followed that these agencies were manned by administrators who were trained in these practices. These principles were based on colonial heritage of restricting native participation, distrusting the common citizen, and enabling an elite group to frame rules and regulations to implement policies. The result was that the inherited administrative system got strengthened, weakening any desire to reform it.[1]

The continuity in the higher civil service coming down from the colonial days led to its members becoming strong beneficiaries of the system and thus began to act as a powerful source of resistance to change. These civil servants came from elite backgrounds and did not have much connect with the poor or rural society. We have already pointed out that the early political leadership took the support of civil servants (initially of the ICS variety) in running many of their flagship programmes. This dependence led to hesitation in rubbing them the wrong way.

But a way had to be found to fulfill the demands of the political leadership which may be in conflict with the rules and regulations set by the administrative system. The administrative system having entrenched itself, we hypothesize that it moulded itself to the kind we have described earlier. Ninan (2015: 141) argues that the business

---

[1] The Seventh Pay Commission that submitted its report in November 2015 could not resolve the issue of reducing the primacy of IAS in the government services, which was a strong demand of other services that were more specialized in nature.

of administration remains largely unreformed because no politician wants to take on organized groups. Whatever reform takes place is, therefore, usually designed to leave existing administrative structures alone to create new institutions to take on new roles.

Political leadership then becomes adept at bending the administrative system rather than reforming it, and its disconnect with the common citizens helps a lot in this process. Elections are held and voters are wooed, but leaders once elected lose interest in them. Empowering them is seen as a threat to their own power and patronage. Administrative reform that would make the government responsive, accountable, and lead to simplification of procedures that would help the poor to get their entitlements was seen precisely at doing that.

There is another striking feature of the administrative scene in India. As we have narrated in the earlier chapters, efforts at administrative reforms proposed by government experts and committees did not fructify. This happened in spite of public outcry against administrative inefficiencies, corruption, and poor performance of schemes and projects that were particularly targeted for the benefit of the poor. Little social mobilization to strengthen or force government hands to reform administration took place. Political and administrative leadership would make a plea for reform but would not do much. Large businesses took little interest in a systemic reform as long as individual benefits continued to accrue to them.

In recent years, however, two mass mobilizations to make the administration accountable to the people did take place. One was seeking greater transparency in the system and the other for the appointment of lokpal. The transparency movement did have some success and the RTI Act was enacted in 2005. The appointment of lokpal is in a limbo. After considerable negotiations and bargaining over its content, a bill has been passed by Parliament and the law has been notified. But no further action has been taken and the institution is yet to take off. Both these public efforts were directed more at accountability of an administrative system that was perceived as autocratic and impervious to public needs. They were not directly pressurizing the government for administrative reform. Undoubtedly, democratic accountability is critical and may ultimately lead to administrative reform. But the experience of the working of the transparency law has not given that kind of hope.

New governance institutions are being superimposed on an administrative system that has been unresponsive to the state goals and policy environment. Even though informed by the principles of privatization, these new institutions have to work with the existing administrative system whose characteristics of inflexibility have been taken up in earlier discussion. But if capacities of the existing administration are not improved when it comes to setting of rules, regulations, and principles of supervision and dispute settlement, including those of project execution and service provision, the country is setting itself up for more systemic failures (Ninan 2015: 81–2). It appears that effort towards administrative reforms now needs to be on an even higher priority than before.

Governance reforms, in essence, are introducing a new mode of delivering public services and transforming the way in which public interest is pursued. This is presenting a major challenge, for shedding of traditional governmental functions is being taken up with great enthusiasm. Two kinds of developments are taking place in this process.

One is that the new institutions that are being established reflect the so-called experience in OECD countries. International agencies are having considerable influence on Indian policy-making process to adopt these institutions. Semi-autonomous institutions are multiplying in the British administration, while privatization of government functions and introducing PPPs has become the new mantra for implementing public programmes. The role of international donor agencies such as the World Bank and the ADB (as shown earlier) is quite discernible on this count. Large consultancy firms that have been increasingly employed as consultants in the government have also played their role in bringing their ideas of new public management.[2] India has already gone through an earlier experience when recommendations such as performance budgeting, O and M, coming from Western experience and transplanted on the conventional administration, did not take root. Even though the role of institutions in development is well recognized, transfer of institutional knowledge from one country system to another has not been easy.

Already, private sector investment through the PPP route is floundering. In a meeting with the economic affairs secretary, Government of India, a committee to look into difficulties pointed out by representatives of industries has been set up and its recommendations are being examined by the government (*Business Standard* 27 October 2015). These difficulties lie primarily in the interface of the perspectives of the conventional administration and private sector interests. In the meantime, the CAG of India has passed some strictures in the way some of the infrastructure projects were handled (*The Hindu* 19 July 2014).

The other development in the landscape of public administration in India is the emergence of independent regulatory agencies to oversee the performance of these new institutions in the pursuit of public interest. As privatization of public services goes unabated, the concern about its ability to serve public interests also rises. Regulatory agencies are multiplying and being demanded where they do not exist.

The Second Administrative Reforms Commission points out that traditional departmental structures are not suited to play the dual role of policymaking as well as regulating the sector concerned. Independent regulatory agencies are being set up that are

---

[2] The global spread of the ideas of reinventing government and the role of consultants has been elaborated in Saint-Martin (2001).

autonomous of the government and are staffed by experts who have domain knowledge. Such agencies have already come in the sectors of power, telecom, financial services and insurance, and so on. It has been pointed out that these have been promoted by international donor agencies and have been viewed primarily as a mechanism to insulate decision-making processes from politics. It is further suggested these agencies have entered India through the back door and act as one more layer of the government.

Scholars quoted earlier further point out that regulating agencies have been caught between the technical demands, financial health of the sector, consumer dissatisfaction arising from rising tariffs, and the intervention of the government to balance the conflicting interests. They have given in to government encroaching on their terrain for they have been ill-placed to resolve these issues and have merely maintained a facade of independent decision-making.

The neat government in which the minister was held accountable to an elected Parliament for the administration in her charge is not that neat anymore, democracy is celebrated only so long as it holds elections on a regular basis. A consequence of many of these developments is that the whole fabric of democratic accountability, so familiar in a participatory system of government, is fading. The new structures are deemed democratic because they are accountable to their stakeholders and beneficiaries of the specific service provided. Critically, citizens are being converted into stakeholders and customers of services. A new institutional architecture for public administration is emerging in which democracy and public accountability appear as a casualty and citizenship is being reinvented.

Annexure 1 (a)

Setting the Stage for Reforms in the Neoliberal Era[*]
Some Excerpts from the Eighth Five-Year Plan, 1992–7

The Eighth Plan will have to undertake re-examination and reorientation of the role of the Government as well as the process of planning. It will have to work out the ways and means of involving people in the developmental task and social evolution. It will have to strengthen the people's participatory institutions. In keeping with these objectives, the process of planning will have to be re-oriented so as to make planning largely indicative. This, in turn, will imply a somewhat changed role for the Planning Commission. The Planning Commission will have to concentrate on anticipating future trends and evolve integrated strategies for achieving the highest possible level of development of the country in keeping with the internationally competitive standards. In place of the resource allocation role which very largely characterized the working of the Planning Commission in the past, it will have to concentrate on optimal utilization of the limited available resources. This will call for the creation of a culture of high productivity and cost efficiency in the Government both at the Centre and the States and the Planning Commission will have to play the role of a change

[*] The chapter numbers have been retained as per the original report.

agent. At the same time, it must provide the broad blue-print for achieving the essential social and economic objectives and indicate the directions in which the economy and the various sub-sectors should be moving. It should pin-point areas in which advance action should be taken to avoid serious bottlenecks. Planning must thus proceed from a vision of the society to be created, and through an appropriate mix of policy instruments influence the decisions of the various economic agencies to achieve the desired goals. In this sense, indicative planning is a more difficult exercise.

1.1.6 The Eighth Plan is being launched at a time which marks a turning point in both international and domestic economic environment. All over the world centralised economies are disintegrating. On the other hand, economies of several regions are getting integrated under a common philosophy of growth, guided by the market forces and liberal policies. The emphasis is on autonomy and efficiency induced by competition. We cannot remain untouched by these trends. We have to draw lessons from the development experience of other nations during the last four decades. Development economics was largely theoretical when India started her planning in 1951. It has now acquired considerable empirical knowledge based on the rich applied experience of many nations, among whom there are success stories as also failures. Indian planning needs to draw on some of these lessons. It also needs to be guided by its own experience, gained during the last four decades. If planning has to retain its relevance, it must be willing to make appropriate mid-course corrections and adjustments. In that process, it may be necessary to shed off some of the practices and precepts of the past which have outlived their utility and to adopt new practices and precepts, in the light of the experience gained by us and by other nations.

1.4.43 Our experience of development planning has shown that developmental activities undertaken with people's active participation have a greater chance of success and can also be more cost-effective as compared to the development activities undertaken by the Government where people become passive observers. The non-involvement of people has also led to the implantation in them of an attitude of total dependence on government for everything so that there has been a lack of effort by the people and lack of accountability to the people in the system of administering developmental schemes.

1.4.44 In the Eighth Five Year plan, it is necessary to make development a people's movement. People's initiative and participation must become the key element in the whole process of development. A lot in the area of education (especially literacy), health, family planning, land improvement, efficient land use, minor irrigation, watershed management, recovery of wastelands, afforestation, animal husbandry, dairy, fisheries and sericulture etc. can be achieved by creating people's institutions accountable to the community. Therefore the focus of attention will be on developing multiple institutional options for improving the delivery systems by using the vast potential of the voluntary sector.

1.4.45 Importance of decentralised local level planning and people's participation has been recognised. Yet results achieved so far have not been very impressive. In this plan, therefore a new direction is being given to achieve these objectives. So far, the approach to people's participation consisted in programme-based strategies. In addition to such programmes the Planning Commission has now worked out institutional strategies which will mean creating or strengthening various people's institutions at the district, block and village level's so that they synthesise the purpose of investment envisaged in the Plan with optimisation of benefits at the grassroots level by relating these programmes to the needs of people. This can only be achieved through the collective wisdom of the community combined with the latest know-how available. This work is primarily to be undertaken through NGOs with the support of Government.

1.4.46 Various models of people's institutions have been functioning successfully in the country. Studies show that effective institutions have the following essential ingredients:

(a) They are owned and managed by the users/stake holders, producers or beneficiaries themselves;
(b) They are accountable to the community;
(c) They have the capacity to become self-reliant over a period of time;
(d) They have the capacity to diagnose the needs of the areas, inter-act with the governmental agencies in order to draw need-based local level plans and to implement those plans in close cooperation with the administration; and
(e) They tend to bring about integration of various segments of the society for the achievement of common goals of development.

1.4.47 The role of the government should be to facilitate the process of people's involvement in developmental activities by creating the right type of institutional infrastructure, particularly in rural areas. These institutions are very weak particularly in those States where they are needed the most for bringing about an improvement in the socio-demographic indicators. Encouraging voluntary agencies as well as schools, colleges and universities, to get them involved in social tasks and social mobilisation, strengthening of the Panchayat Raj institutions, people orientation and integration of all the village-level programmes under the charge of the Panchayat Raj institutions, and helping the cooperatives to come up in the organisation and support of local economic activities, for example, are some of the steps which the Government must earnestly initiate. A genuine push towards decentralisation and people's participation has become necessary.

Annexure 1 (b)

Changing Policy Perspectives on Governance[*]

Some Excerpts from the Fifth Central Pay Commission Report

CORE FUNCTIONS OF GOVERNMENT

4.5 Contemporaneously, there is no one who advocates on all pervasive role for Government. The attempt is to identify the core functions. There is a fair amount of consensus that the following areas fall within the legitimate province of Government as such:

 (i) National Security
 (ii) International Relations
(iii) Law and Order
(iv) Management of Economy at Macro Level
 (v) Setting up of Infrastructure
(vi) Social Services
(vii) Programmes for Disadvantaged Sections

[*] Vinod Mehta (ed.), *Reforming Administration in India* (New Delhi: Indian Council of Social Science Research and Har-Anand Publishers, 2000), Appendix I, 'Recommendations of Fifth Pay Commission Relating to Administrative Reforms'.

What Government Should Not Do

4.6 At the same time it is recognised that there are functions currently performed by government which ought to be given up. Direct participation in manufacturing, mining and economic services and direct control of economic activity in the private sector are two such major areas. Many countries have divested themselves of public sector enterprises which could be better run in the private sector in the area of coal, steel, fertilizers, air, rail and road transport, tourism, hotelering, banking, insurance and so on. Some countries have turned to the private sector even in the traditionally super-sensitive area of atomic energy, space and defence production. Where some activities have been retained in Government, they have been hived off into separate autonomous agencies with independence of functioning.

State in Relation to Private Sector

4.7 The nature of Government regulation of economic activity has undergone a major change. Governments no longer insist on the issue of licenses and permits for setting up of new industrial units or expansion of existing ones. It is considered wiser to set up autonomous regulating agencies with quasi-judicial powers, in order to ensure that the functioning of private units is regulated in social interest.

Self-governing Institutions

4.12 Secondly, self-governing institutions where the people themselves take over the functions of the State would have to be encouraged, sustained and nurtured. These would include municipal bodies, panchayats, cooperatives, voluntary organizations and the like. Political and administrative authority would necessarily have to be delegated to them. Politicians and bureaucrats, who have traditionally looked at these organizations with contempt or disgust, would have to willingly share power with them.

Annexure 2

TABLE A2.1   Cadre Strength of IAS (as on 1 January 2017)

S. No.	Cadre/States	Strength
1.	Andhra Pradesh	170
2.	AG MUT	279
3.	Assam–Meghalaya	221
4.	Bihar	243
5.	Chhattisgarh	241
6.	Gujarat	178
7.	Haryana	155
8.	Himachal Pradesh	115
9.	Jammu and Kashmir	91
10.	Jharkhand	144
11.	Karnataka	215
12.	Kerala	150
13.	Madhya Pradesh	341
14.	Maharashtra	313
15.	Manipur	91
16.	Nagaland	67
17.	Odisha	178
18.	Punjab	182
19.	Rajasthan	243
20.	Sikkim	37
21.	Tamil Nadu	289
22.	Telangana	130
23.	Tripura	76
24.	Uttarakhand	87
25.	Uttar Pradesh	515
26.	West Bengal	277
	Total	**5,004**

Source: Available at civillist.ias.nic.in/YrCurr/PDF/CadreStrength01012017.pdf, last accessed on 5 October 2017.

Annexure 3

TABLE A3.1   Attractiveness of Civil Service

	2012–13	2013–14	2014–15
No. of Applicants, Preliminary Exam	550,080	776,604	947,428
No. of Applicants, Main Exam	12,795	14,800	16,706
No. Appeared in Main Exam	12,190	14,178	16,286
No. of Candidates Interviewed	2,415	2,669	3,001
Recommended	999	998	1,122

Source: Government of India, *Report of the Civil Services Examination Review Committee* (Alagh Committee) (New Delhi, Union Public Service Commission, 2001).

Annexure 4

TABLE A4.1 Schemes and Modalities of PPPs

Schemes	Modalities
Build–own–operate (BOO) Build–develop–operate (BDO) Design–construct–manage–finance (DCMF)	The private sector designs, builds, owns, develops, operates and manages an asset with no obligation to transfer ownership to the government. These are variants of design-build-finance-operate (DBFO) schemes.
Buy–build–operate (BBO) Lease–develop–operate (LDO) Wrap-around addition (WAA)	The private sector buys or leases an existing asset from the Government, renovates, modernizes, and/or expands it, and then operates the asset, again with no obligation to transfer owner-ship back to the Government.
Build–operate–transfer (BOT) Build–own–operate–transfer (BOOT) Build–rent–own–transfer (BROT) Build–lease–operate–transfer (BLOT) Build–transfer–operate (BTO)	The private sector designs and builds an asset, operates it, and then transfers it to the Government when the operating contract ends, or at some other pre-specified time. The private partner may subsequently rent or lease the asset from the Government.

Source: V. Lakkshamanan, 'Public–Private Partnership in Indian Infrastructure Development: Issues and Options', *Reserve Bank of India Occasional Papers* 29, no. 1 (2008): 37–77.

References

Ahuja, Sanjeev K. 27 January 2010. *Highway Body to Widen NH-8*. *Hindustan Times*.

Ananth, V. Krishna. 2011. 'Lokpal Bill Campaign: Democratic and Constitutional'. *Economic and Political Weekly* 46, no. 16.

Appleby, Paul. 1953. *Public Administration in India Report of a Survey*. Delhi, Government of India.

Arora, Ramesh K. 2015. *District Collectors Recollections and Reflections*. Jaipur, Paragon International Publishers.

Asian Development Bank. 2006. *Facilitating Public–Private Partnership for Accelerated Infrastructure Development Regional Workshops of Chief Secretaries on Public Private Partnership Workshop Report*. New Delhi.

Bagal, Satish. 2008. 'Managing Public–Private Partnerships'. *Economic and Political Weekly* 43, no. 33: 23–6.

Bagchi, Sanjoy. 2007. *The Changing Face of Bureaucracy*. Delhi, Rupa and Co.

Bakker, Karen. 2011. *Privatizing Water Governance Failure and the World's Urban Water Crisis*. New Delhi, Orient BlackSwan.

Baldwin, Robert et al. 2013. *Understanding Regulation Theory, Strategy and Practice*. Oxford, Oxford University Press.

Banik, Dan. 2001. 'The Transfer Raj: Indian Civil Servants on the Move'. *The European Journal Development Research* 13, no. 1: 106–34.

Bardhan, P. 1984. *The Political Economy of Development in India*. Delhi, Oxford University Press.

Bhambhri, C.P. 1972. *Administrators in a Changing Society*. New Delhi, National Publishing House.

Bhattacharya, A. K. 4 October 2015. 'Winds of Change'. *Times of India*.

Bhattacharya, Saugata and Urjit R. Patel. 2005. 'New Regulatory Institutions in India: White Knights or Trojan Horses'. In *Public Institutions in India Performance and Design*, edited by Devesh Kapur and Pratap Bhanu Mehta, 406–56. Delhi, Oxford University Press.

Bjorkman, J.W. 1979. *Politics of Administrative Alienation in India's Rural Development Programmes*. Delhi, Ajanta Publications.

Braibanti, Ralph. 1966. 'Transnational Inducement of Administrative Reform'. In *Approaches to Development, Politics and Change*, edited by J.D. Montgomery and W.J. Siffin, 133–83. New York, McGraw-Hill.

Business Standard. 22 May 2013; 27 October 2015; 8 February 2016; 5 April 2018.

Chakrabarty, Bidyut and Mohit Bhattacharya. 2008. *The Governance Discourse A Reader.* New Delhi, Oxford University Press.

Chandavarkar, Rajnarayan. 2007. 'Customs of Governance: Colonialism and Democracy in Twentieth Century India'. *Modern Asian Studies* 41, no. 3: 441–70.

Chandhoke, Neera. 2007. 'Engaging with Civil Society: The Democratic Perspective Prepared for the Non-Government Public Action'. Programme Directed by Professor Jude Howell Centre for Civil Society, London School of Economics and Political Science.

Chandler, Ralph C. and Jack C. Plano. 1988. *The Public Administration Dictionary*. Santa Barbara, ABC-Clio.

Chandrashekhar, Lalita. 2011. *Undermining Local Democracy Parallel Governance in Contemporary South India*. New Delhi, Routledge.

Chaturvedi, H.R. 1977. *Bureaucracy and the Local Community: Dynamics of Rural Development*. Bombay, Allied Publishers.

Chaturvedi, M.K. 1971. 'Commitment in Civil Service'. *Indian Journal of Public Administration* 17, no. 1: 40–6.

Chaturvedi, T.N. 1964. 'Tensions in Panchayati Raj: Relations between Officials and Non-Officials'. *Economic Weekly* 15, no. 22: 36–7.

Chauhan, Chetan. 2 March 2011. 'Citizens May Get RTI Information for PPP Projects'. *Hindustan Times*.

Chettur, S.K. 1964. *The Steel Frame and I*. Bombay, Asia Publishing House.

Chhotray, V. 2012. *The Anti-Politics Machine in India State, Decentralization and Participatory Watershed Development*. UK, Anthem Press.

'Committed Civil Service: A Symposium'. August 1973. *Seminar* 168.

Cohn, Jonathan. 25 October 1999. 'Irrational Exuberance. When Did Political Science Forget about Politics'. *The New Republic.* Available at www.nuff.ox.ac.uk/users/Kayser/TNR Cohn.pdf

Dar, R.K., ed. 1998. *Governance and the IAS in Search of Resilience.* New Delhi, Tata McGraw Hill.

Dardot, Pierre and Christian Laval. 2013. *The New Way of the World on Neo-Liberal Society.* Translated by Gergory Elliott. London, Versova.

Das, Gurcharan. 2000. *India Unbound.* New Delhi, Penguin India.

Das, S.K. 1998. *Civil Service Reform and Structural Adjustment.* Delhi, Oxford University. Press

————. 2001. *Public Office, Private Interest Bureaucracy and Corruption in India.* New Delhi, Oxford University Press.

————. 2005. 'Institutions of Internal Accountability'. In *Public Institutions in India Performance and Design,* edited by Devesh Kapur and Pratap Bhanu Mehta. Delhi, Oxford University Press.

Dash, Dipak K. 25 December 2014. 'Stung by CAG Censure NHAI, Says Auditor Does Not Understand PPP Concept'. *Times of India.*

Datta, Amrita. 2009. 'Public–Private Partnerships in India'. *Economic and Political Weekly* 44, no. 33: 73–8.

Davies, William. 2014. *The Limits of Neo-liberalism Authority, Sovereignty and the Logic of Competition.* London and New York, SAGE Publishers.

Dearra, G. and Patrick Plane. 2014. 'Assessing the World Bank's Influence on the Good Governance Paradigm'. *Oxford Development Studies* 42, no. 4: 473–87.

Deccan Herald. 13 September 2011.

Dhar, T.N. 2006. 'Good Governance, Civil Service Reforms and Decentralization'. *Indian Journal of Public Administration Special Number on Excellence in Public Service* 52: 448–58.

Doornbos, Martin. 2001. '"Good Governance": The Rise and Decline of Policy Metaphor'. *Journal of Development Studies* 37, no. 6: 93–108.

Dorey, Peter. 2005. *Policy Making in Britain: An Introduction.* London, SAGE Publications.

Dubash, N.K. March 2012. 'Regulating through the Backdoor: Understanding the Implications of Institutional Transplant'. Jerusalem Papers in Regulation and Governance, Working paper no. 42.

Dubash Navroz K. and Morgan B. *The Rise of the Regulatory State of the South.* Oxford, Oxford University Press.

————. 2012. 'Understanding the Rise of Regulating State of the South'. *Regulation and Governance* 6: 261–81.

Dubhashi, P.R. 1971 'Committed Bureaucracy'. *Indian Journal of Public Administration* 17, no. 1: 33–9.

Dwivedi Gaurav, Rahmat and Dharmadhikari Sripad. 2007. *Water. Private, Limited Issues in Privatization, Corporatization and Commercialization of Water Sector in India.* Barwani, M.P., Manthan Adyan Kendra, revised edition.

Dwivedi, O.P. and Kieth M. Henderson. 1990. *Public Administration World Perspective.* Ames, Iowa State University Press.

Economic Times, The. 21 August 2015; 14 September 2017.

Fukuyama, Francis. 2004. *State Building Governance and World Order in the Twentieth Century.* London, Profile Books.

————. 2014. *Political Order and Political Decay from the Industrial Revolution to the Globalization of Democracy.* New York, Straus and Giroux.

Gaikwad, V.R. 1969. *Panchayati Raj and Bureaucracy: A Study of Relationship Patterns.* Hyderabad, National Institute of Community Development.

Gandhi, Shailesh. 2015. 'State of the RTI Regime in India'. In *Empowerment Through Information: The Evolution of Transparency Regimes in South Asia.* Vol. 1: *Essays, Status Reports and Case Studies,* edited by Shamsul Bari, Vikram K. Chand, and Shekhar Singh. Delhi, TAG and RIB.

Gant, George. 1979. *Development Administration: Concepts, Goals and Methods.* Madison, University of Wisconsin Press.

Goldman, Michel. 2007. 'How Water for All Policy Became Hegemonic: The Power of the World Bank and Its Transnational Networks'. *Geoforum* 38: 786–800. Available at www.sciencedirect.com.

Gopalaswami, Ayyangar N. 1949. *Report on Reorganization of the Machinery of Government.* New Delhi, Government of India.

Gorwala, A.D. 1951. *Report on Public Administration.* New Delhi, Planning Commission Government of India.

Government of India. 1978. *Report of the Committee on Panchayati Raj Institutions.* New Delhi.

————. 1996. *Report of the Fifth Central Pay Commission.* New Delhi, Ministry of Finance.

————. 1997. *Working Group on Right to Information and Promotion of Open and Transparent Government* (chairman, H.D. Shourie). New Delhi, Department of Personnel.

————. 2001. *Report of the Civil Services Examination Review Committee* (Alagh Committee). New Delhi, Union Public Service Commission.

————. 2002. *National Water Policy Ministry of Water Resources.* New Delhi.

————. 2008. *PPPs Creating an Enabling Environment for State Projects.* Delhi, Ministry of Finance, Department of Economic Affairs.

————. 2015a. *Report of the Committee on Revisiting and Revitalizing Public–Private Partnership Model for Infrastructure* (Kelkar Committee). New Delhi, Ministry of Finance.

————. 2015b. *Report of the Seventh Central Pay Commission.* Delhi, Ministry of Finance.

————. 2016. *PPP Guide for Practitioners.* New Delhi, Department of Economic Affairs, Ministry of Finance.

Guha, R. 2007. *India After Gandhi The History of World's Largest Democracy.* London, MacMillan.

————, ed. 2014. *Makers of Modern Asia.* Cambridge Mass and London, The Bellknap Press of Harvard University Press.

Gupta, A. 2015. 'Emerging Trends in Higher Education in India'. In *India Higher Education Report*, edited by N.V. Varghese and Garima Malik. New York, Routledge.

Hajer, Maartin A. and Hendrik Wagenaar. 2003. *Deliberative Policy Analysis Understanding Governance in Network Society.* Cambridge, Cambridge University Press.

Hay, Colin. 2004. 'Theory Stylized Heuristic or Self-fulfilling Prophecy the Status of Rational Choice Theory in Public Administration'. *Public Administration* 82, no. 1: 39–62.

Hay, Colin and David Richards. 2000. 'The Tangled Web of Westminster and Whitehall: The Discourse Strategy and Practice of Networking within the British Core Executive'. *Public Administration* 78, no. 1: 1–28.

Hindu, The. 19 July 2014; 2 September 2017.

Hindu Business Line, The. 5 June 2012.

Hindustan Times, The. December 1969; 10 August 2012; 19 January 2015; 21 October 2015; 1 January 2016; 6 April 2016.

Hirst, P. 1995. 'Quangos and Democratic Government'. *Parliamentary Affairs* 48, no. 2: 341–59.

Hooda, S.K. 2015. 'Changing Pattern of Public Expenditure on Health in India: Issues and Challenges'. Working Paper. New Delhi, ISID.

Indian Express. 11 April 2018. 'Kharge Boycotts Lokpal Meet Again, Writes to PM'.

─────. 29 August 2009; 2011; 24 May 2012; 11 August 2017.

Jagannathan, S. 2001. 'The Role of Non-governmental Organizations in Primary Education: A Study of NGOs in India'. Policy research working paper no. 2530. Washington, DC, World Bank.

Jain, R.B. 2000. 'New Directions in Administrative Reform in India'. In *Reforming Administration in India*, edited by Vinod Mehta. New Delhi: ICSSR, Har-Anand Publications.

Johri, Amrita, Anjali Bhardwaj, and Shekhar Singh. 1 February 2014. 'The Lokpal Act of 2014: An Assessment'. *Economic and Political Weekly* 49, no. 5: 10–13.

Kapur, Devesh and Pratap Bhanu Mehta, eds. 2003. *Public Institutions in India Performance and Design*. Delhi, Oxford University Press.

Kaul, V.N. 2012. 'CAG and the Mandate Question'. In *Contemporary Issues in Public Accountability and Audit*, edited by M.M. Mathur, Vir Dharam, and T. Sethumadhavan, 33–40. New Delhi, Institute of Public Auditors of India.

Kochanek, Stanley A. 1987. 'Briefcase Politics in India: The Congress Party and the Business Elite'. *Asian Survey* 27, no. 12: 1278–301.

─────. 1996. 'Liberalization and Business Lobbying in India'. *Pacific Affairs* 34, no. 3: 155–73.

Kohli, Atul. 2006. 'Politics of Economic Growth in India 1980–2005', Part 1: 'The 1980s' and Part 2: 'The 1990s and Beyond'. *Economic and Political Weekly*: 1251–9 and 1361–70.

Kothari, S. and Ramashray Roy. 1969. *Relations between Politicians and Administrators at the District Level*. New Delhi, Indian Institute of Public Administration.

LaPalombara, J., ed. 1963. *Bureaucracy and Political Development*. Princeton, Princeton University Press.

Lakkshamanan, V. 2008. 'Public–Private Partnership in Indian Infrastructure Development: Issues and Options'. *Reserve Bank of India Occasional Papers* 29, no. 1: 37–77.

Lane, Jan Eric. 2000. *The Public Sector Concepts. Methods and Approaches.* New Delhi, SAGE Publications.

Maheshwari, S.R. 1972. *The Administrative Reforms Commission*. Agra, Laxmi Narain Agarwal.

─────. 1992. *Problems and Issues in Administrative Federalism*. New Delhi, Allied Publishers.

─────. 1993. *Administrative Reform in India*. Delhi, Jawahar Publishers.

Mander, Harsh and Abha Joshi. 1999. 'The Movement for Right to Information in India People's Power for the Control of Corruption'. Paper presented at the Conference in Pan Commonwealth Advocacy, 21–4 January.

Manning, Nick. 2001. 'The Legacy of the New Public Administration in Developing Countries'. *International Review of Administrative Sciences* 67: 297–312.

Mathur, B.P. 2005. *Governance Reform for Vision India*. New Delhi, MacMillan.

———. 2014. *Ethics for Governance Reinventing Public Services*. New Delhi, Routledge.

Mathur, Kuldeep. 1972a. *Bureaucratic Response to Development*. Delhi, National Publishing House.

———. 1972b. *Sources of Indian Bureaucratic Behaviour Organizational Environment and Political Processes in Rajasthan*. Jaipur, HCM State Institute of Public Administration.

———. 1982. *Bureaucracy and the New Agricultural Strategy*. New Delhi, Concept Pub.

———. 1991. 'Bureaucracy in India: Development and Pursuit of Self-Interest'. *Indian Journal of Public Administration* 37, no. 4: 637–48.

———. 2003. 'Privatization as Reform Liberalization and Public Enterprises in India'. In *The Public and the Private Issues of Democratic Citizenship*, edited by Gurpreet Mahajan. New Delhi, SAGE Publications.

———. 2006. 'Empowering Local Government Decentralization and Governance'. In *India's Social Development Report*, edited by Amitabh Kundu. New Delhi, Council for Social Development and Oxford University Press.

———. 2012. *Panchayati Raj*. Oxford India Short Introductions. Delhi, Oxford University Press.

———. 2013. *Panchayti Raj*. New Delhi, Oxford University Press.

———. 2015. 'Evolution of RTI Regime in India Broadening of the Dominant Narrative'. In *Empowerment Through Information:The Evolution of Transparency Regimes in South Asia*, edited by Shamsul Bari,Vikram K. Chand, and Shekhar Singh, 40–61. New Delhi,Transparency Advisory Group.

Mathur, Kuldeep, Bhavna Thakur, Pooja Ravi, and Richa Singh. 2013. *Public–Private Partnership and Public Accountability*. New Delhi, Centre for Democracy and Social Development.

Mathur, Nayanika and Laura Bear. 2015. 'Remaking the Public Good: A New Anthropology of Bureaucracy'. *The Cambridge Journal Anthropology* 33, no. 1: 18–34.

Mathur, Navdeep and Chris Skelcher. 2007. 'Evaluating Democratic Performance Methodologies for Assessing the Relationship between Network Citizen and Citizen'. *Public Administration Review* 2, no. 67: 228–37.

Mathur, M.M., Dharam Vir, and T. Setumadhavan (editorial team). 2012. *Contemporary Issues in Public Accountability and Audit*. New Delhi, Institute of Public Auditors of India and APH Publishing House.

Mehta, Anouj, Aparna Bhatia, and Ameeta Chatterjee. 2010. *Improving Health and Education Service Delivery in India Public-Private Partnership*. ADB-Government of India Initiative, ADB, Manila. Available at health-education-delivery-india-ppp-adb-dea(1).pdf.

Mehta, Vinod, ed. 2000. *Reforming Administration in India*. New Delhi, Indian Council of Social Science Research and Har-Anand Publishers.

Miller Hugh, T. and Charles J. Fox. 2007. *Post Modern Public Administration*. New York, ME Sharpe, revised edition.

Minogue, Martin, Charles Polidano, and David Hume. 1998. *Beyond the New Public Management Changing Ideas and Practices in Governance*. Chettenham, Edward Elgar.

Mint, The. 16 June 2014.

Mohapatra, Atanu. 2013. 'Lokpal and the Role of Media in Propping up Anti-Corruption Movement in India'. *International Journal of Social Science and Inter-Disciplinary Research* 2, no. 3: 42–53.

Mohr, Alison. 2004. *Public–Private Partnerships Gaining Efficiency at the Cost of Public Accountability*. International Summer Academy on Technology Studies—Urban Infrastructure in Transition (Archives). Available at https://www.researchgate.net/publication/255626294_Governance_through_public_private_partnerships_Gaining_efficiency_at_the_cost_of_public_accountability.

Mookerjee, Nivedita. 5 April 2018. 'Know Thy PMO: How Powerful Is the Office Really and How Does it Function?' *Business Standard*.

Mukherjee, Mithi. 2010. *India in the Shadows of Empire: A Legal and Political History 1774–1950*. Delhi, Oxford University Press.

Murali, Kanta. 2017. *Caste, Class and Capital: The Social and Political Origins of Economic Policy in India*. Delhi, Cambridge University Press.

Nehru, Jawaharlal. 1953. *An Autobiography*. Oxford, Oxford University Press.

Ninan, T.N. 2015. *The Turn of the Tortoise: The Challenge and Promise of India's Future*. Gurgaon, Allen Lane (Penguin Group).

Offe, Claus. 2009. 'Governance: An Empty Signifier'. *Constellations* 16, no. 4: 551–61.

Osborne, David and Ted Gaebler. 1992. *Reinventing Government: How the Entrepreneurial Spirit Is Transforming the Public Sector from Schoolhouse to Statehouse, City Hall to Pentagon*. New Delhi, Prentice-Hall of India.

Ostrom, V. and Elinor Ostrom. 1971. 'Public Choice: A Different Approach to the Study of Public Administration'. *Public Administration Review* 31, no. 2: 203–16.

Pai, Panandiker and S.S. Kshirsagar. 1978. *Bureaucracy and Development Administration*. New Delhi, Centre for Policy Research.

Panagriya, A. 2008. *India: The Emerging Giant*. Oxford, Oxford University Press.

Peters, Guy B. 2003. 'The Changing Nature of Public Administration'. *International Review of Administrative Sciences* 5: 7–20.

Pierre, Jon, ed. 2000. *Debating Governance*. Oxford, Oxford University Press.

———. 2009a. *Why Legality Matters: The Limits of Markets and Governance Reform in the Public Sector*. QoG Working Paper Series. Gothenborg, University of Gothenburg.

———. 2009b. *We Are All Customers Now: Understanding the Influence of Economic Theory on Public Adminsitration*. QoG Working Paper Series. Gothenburg, The Quality of Government Institute University of Gothenburg.

Pingle, Vibha. 2000. *Rethinking the Developmental State: India's Industry in Comparative Perspective*. Delhi, Oxford University Press.

Potter, David C. 1986. *India's Political Administrators 1919–83*. Oxford, Clarendon Press.

Prakash, Arun. 13 September 2017. 'Agenda for Raksha Mantri'. *Indian Express*.

Pritchette, Lant, Michael Woolcock, and Matt Andrews. 2010. *Capability Traps? The Mechanisms of Persistent Implementation Failure*. Washington, DC, Center for Global Development.

Punjabi, K.L., ed. 1965. *Civil Servant in India*. Bombay, Bhartiya Vidya Bhawan.

RAAG. *People's Monitoring of the RTI Regime in India*. New Delhi, 2016.

Raghavan, Srinath. 2014. 'Indira Gandhi, India and the World in Transition'. In *Makers of Modern Asia*, edited by Ramachandra Guha.

Cambridge, Mass, and London, The Bellknap Press of Harvard University Press.

Ravindran, T.K.S. 2011. 'Public-Private Partnerships in Maternal Health Services'. *Economic and Political Weekly* 47, no. 48: 43–52.

Reddy, P.L. Sanjeev, Jaideep Singh, and R.K. Tiwari, eds. 2004. *Democracy, Governance and Globalization Essays in Honour of Paul H. Appleby*. New Delhi, Indian Institute of Public Administration.

Reijners, J.J.A.M. 1994. 'Organization of Public–Private Partnerships Projects: The Timely Prevention of Pitfalls'. *International Journal of Project Management* 12, no. 3: 137–40.

Riggs, F.W. 1965. 'Bureaucrats and Political Development: A Paradoxical View'. In *Bureaucracy and Political Development*, edited by J. LaPalombara. Princeton, NJ, Princeton University Press.

—————. 1976 'The Group and the Movement: Notes on Comparative and Development Administration'. *Public Administration Review* 36, no. 6: 648–54.

—————. 1998. 'Public Administration in America: Why Our Uniqueness Is Exceptional and Important'. *Public Administration Review* 58, no. 1: 22–31.

Rhodes, R.A.W. 2006. 'Policy Network Analysis'. In *The Oxford Handbook of Public Policy*, edited by M. Moran, M. Rein, and R. Goodin, 425–47. Oxford, Oxford University Press.

Roberts Alasdair. 2010. *The Logic of Discipline Global Capitalism and the Architecture of Government*. Oxford, Oxford University Press.

Rosen, George. 1985. *Western Economists and Eastern Societies Agents of Change in South Asia 1950–1970*. Delhi, Oxford University Press.

Rosenau, P.V. 2000. *Public-Private Partnerships*. Cambridge, MIT Press.

Roy, Aruna, Nkhil Dey, and Shanker Singh. April 2001. 'Demanding Accountability'. *Seminar*.

Rudolph, L.I. and Rudolph S.H. 1987. *In Pursuit of Lakshmi: The Political Economy of India State*. Hyderabad, Orient Longman.

—————. 2003. 'The State and Its Permanent Government'. In *Public Administration: A Reader*, edited by Chakravarty B. and M. Bhattacharya. Delhi, Oxford University Press.

Saint-Martin, D. 2001. 'How the Reinventing Government Movement in Public Administration Was Exported from the US to Other Countries'. *International Journal of Public Administration* 24, no. 6: 573–604.

Saxena, A.P. 2004. 'Jawaharlal Nehru and Appleby Reports'. In *Democracy, Governance and Globalization Essays in Honour of Paul H. Appleby*, edited by P.L. Reddy, Sanjeev, Jaideep Singh, and R.K. Tiwari. New Delhi, Indian Institute of Public Administration, 159–87.

Schick, Allen. 1998. 'Why Most Developing Countries Should Not Try New Zealand's Reforms'. *The World Bank Research Observer* 13, no. 1: 123–31.

Scott, James C. 1998. *Seeing Like a State: How Certain Schemes to Improve Human Condition Have Failed*. New Haven, Conn., Yale University Press.

Sebastian, P.T. 26 November 2011. 'Drop the Iron Curtain'. *Business Magazine.* Available at business.outlookindia.com/article.aspx?2279038.

Second Administrative Reforms Commission. 2008. *Refurbishing of Personnel Administration Scaling New Heights*. 10th Report. Delhi, Government of India.

Sharma, Nidhi. 10 January 2011. 'PPP Projects under RTI'. *Economic Times*.

Sharma, Prashant. 2013. *Democracy and Transparency in the India State: The Making of the Right to Information Act*. Edinburgh, Routledge, South Asian Studies Series.

Sharma, Tarun. 3 March 2011. 'Bring PPP under RTI CIC Tells Plan Panel'. *Indian Express*.

Shunglu, V.K. 2012. 'Concept of Accountability and the Role of Supreme Audit Institutions'. In *Contemporary Issues in Public Accountability and Audit*, edited by M.M. Mathur, Vir Dharam, and T. Sethumadhavan, 33–40. New Delhi: Institute of Public Auditors of India.

Singh, Satyajit. 2016. *The Local in Governance Poilitcs, Decentralization and Environment*. New Delhi, Oxford University Press.

Singh, Shekhar. 2011. 'The Genesis and the Evolution of Right to Regime'. In *Transparent Governance in Asia (Background Papers and Proceedings of the Regional Workshop on Towards More Open and Transparent Government in South Asia)*. Delhi, Indian Institute of Public Administration.

Sinha, Aseema. 2005. *The Regional Roots of Development Politics in India: A Divided Leviathan*. Delhi, Oxford University Press.

Slaughter, Anne-Mari. 2004. 'Disaggregated Sovereignty Towards the Public Accountability of Global Government Networks'. *Government and Opposition* 39, no. 2: 159–90.

Sorenson, Eva and Jacob Torfing. 2004. *Making Governance Networks Democratic*. Working Paper 2004:1. Denmark, Centre for Democratic Governance Roskilde. Available at www.demnetgov.ruc.dk.

Spangenburg B. 1976. *British Bureaucracy in India: Status, Policy and the ICS in the Late Nineteenth Century*. Delhi, Manohar Book Service.

Srivastava, Meetika. 2009. 'A Study of Administrative Reforms in India— with Particular Reference to the RTI Act, 2005'. Available at SSRN: http://ssrn.com/abstract=1461773

Stoker, Gerry. 1998. 'Governance as Theory: Five Propositions'. *International Social Science Journal* 155: 18–28.

Streets, Julia. 2004. *Developing a Framework: Concepts and Research Priorities for Partnership Accountability*. Berlin, Global Public Policy Institute. Available at http://globalpublicpolicy.net.

Sundaram, P.S.A. 1997. 'Recent Initiatives for Administrative Reform'. In *Indian Journal of Public Administration Fifty Years of Indian Administration Retrospect and Prospect* 43, no. 3: 553–9.

Sundari Ravindran, T.K. 26 November 2011. 'PPPs in Maternal Health Services'. *Economic and Political Weekly* 46, no. 48: 43–52.

Swaroop, Anand. 6 January 1990. 'Bureaucracy and Politics'. *Times of India*.

Taylor, Carl C., Ensminger Douglas, Johnson Helen, and Joyce Jean. 1966. *India's Roots of Democracy*. New York, Praeger.

Times of India, The. 6 January 1990; 2011; 4 June 2014; 24 June 2015; 4 August 2017; 13 April 2018.

United Nations. 1975. *Development Administration: Current Approaches Trends in Public Administration for National Development*. New York, Department of Economic and Social Affairs, United Nations.

Utting, Peter and Anne Zammit. 2006. *Beyond Pragmatism: Appriasing UN Business Partnerships Markets, Business and Regulation Programme*. Paper no. 1. Geneva, United Nations Research Institute for Social Development.

Van Dyke David, M. 2003. 'The Mythology of Privatization in Contracting Social Services'. *Public Administration Review* 63, no. 3: 296–315.

Venkatraman, A. and J.W. Bjorkman. 2009. *Public–Private Partnerships in Health Care in India*. New York, Routledge.

Wettenhall, Roger. 2006. 'Agencies and Non-Departmental Public Bodies'. *Public Management Review* 7, no. 4: 615–35.

Woodruff, Philip. 1954. *The Men Who Ruled India*. London, Jonathan Cape.

World Bank. 1994. *Governance: The World Bank's Experience*. Washington, DC, World Bank.

Index

accountability 19, 33, 49, 60–1, 63, 85–6, 92–3, 124, 128, 133–5, 144–5; democratic 67, 136, 158, 160
administrative reforms 2, 6, 8, 38–40, 42, 47–8, 50–1, 61, 69, 152–5, 157–8, 161–4
Administrative Reforms Commission (ARC) 2, 20, 26, 28–9, 34–5, 45–52, 87, 106, 138, 153, 159
administrative system 1–2, 7–9, 13–14, 21–2, 24–6, 35, 38–9, 46–7, 51, 54–5, 156–8; characteristic of 19; federal system in 15; Sharma on 79; structures of 9, 14, 44, 157
Advani, L.K. 127
Ahluwalia, Montek Singh 145–7
aid-giving agencies 53, 80
Ambani-Birla Committee 114
Appleby Reports (1953) 43, 45
Appleby, Paul 2, 39, 41–4, 69
Asian Development Bank (ADB) 70, 82, 106–7, 109, 114, 158
Associated Chambers of Commerce and Industry (ASSOCHAM) 98

Bagal, Satish 111
Bagchi, Sanjoy 16, 28

Bardhan, P. 155
Bhandar, Annapurna 112
Bhattacharya, A. K. 36, 64, 87
Bhattacharya, Mohit 64
Bhopal gas tragedy 137
Bhushan, Prashant 148
Boothlingam 23
Braibanti, Ralph 43
British colonial rule 1, 8, 11, 151
bureaucracy, power of 23; Sinha on 4, 13, 23–4, 30, 35–8, 42, 52–5, 58–9, 91–2, 96, 100
bureaucrats 23, 28, 30–1, 33–4, 36, 38, 47, 55, 57–8

central information commissioner (CIC) 143, 145–7
centralization of powers 36
Centre for Civil Society 114
Chakrabarty, Bidyut 64
Chanda, A.K. 125
Chandrashekhar 78, 85
Chhotray 13
civil servants 17, 22–5, 28–9, 31–4, 36–7, 39–40, 54, 105–8, 139, 142, 156
civil society 9, 12, 49, 65–9, 79, 90, 92, 114, 146, 149; activism 141; activists 139; institutions 64–5;

University Grants Commission
    (UGC) 117
Utting, Peter 89

Vajpayee, A.B. 35
voluntary sector 48–9, 114. *See also*
    non-governmental organizations
    (NGOs)

water, privatization of 80
Weberian–Wilsonian framework
    20, 69

Whitehall model 26
Woodruff, Philip 10
World Bank 25, 38, 53, 61–3, 67,
    69–70, 72, 80, 82–3, 107, 114
World Business Council for
    Sustainable Development 80
World Commission on Water 80

Young 115

Zammit, Anne 89

About the Author

Kuldeep Mathur is former professor, Centre for Political Studies, Jawaharlal Nehru University, New Delhi, India. He has also taught at the Indian Institute of Public Administration (IIPA), New Delhi, India. He was earlier rector of Jawaharlal Nehru University and director of National Institute of Education Planning and Administration (NIEPA), New Delhi, India. He has been a member of United Nations Committee of Experts on Public Administration (UNCEPA). He has published on subjects such as public policy processes, bureaucracy, and decentralization. His latest publications include *From Government to Governance: A Brief Survey of the Indian Experience* (2008) and *Public Policy and Politics in India: How Institutions Matter* (Oxford University Press, 2013).